My Brilliant Friends

GENDER AND CULTURE SERIES

GENDER AND CULTURE

A Series of Columbia University Press

Nancy K. Miller and Victoria Rosner, Series Editors

Carolyn G. Heilbrun (1926–2003) and Nancy K. Miller, Founding Editors

For a complete list of books in the series see page 223

My Brilliant Friends

OUR LIVES
IN FEMINISM

Nancy K. Miller

 Columbia University Press *New York*

Columbia University Press
Publishers Since 1893
New York   Chichester, West Sussex
cup.columbia.edu

Library of Congress Cataloging-in-Publication Data
Names: Miller, Nancy K., 1941- author.
Title: My brilliant friends : our lives in feminism / Nancy K. Miller.
Description: New York : Columbia University Press, [2018] |
    Includes bibliographical references.
Identifiers: LCCN 2018022549 (print) | LCCN 2018026082 (e-book) |
    ISBN 9780231548946 (e-book) | ISBN 9780231190541 (cloth : alk. paper)
Subjects: LCSH: Miller, Nancy K., 1941- | Feminism—United States. |
    Female friendship—United States.
Classification: LCC HQ1421 (e-book) | LCC HQ1421 .M55 2018 (print) |
    DDC 305.420973—dc23
LC record available at https://lccn.loc.gov/2018022549

Printed in the United States of America

Cover and interior illustrations by Jojo Karlin
Cover and book design: Lisa Hamm

For Susan Gubar

Contents

The Art of Losing

> As is well known, the ancients thought friends
> indispensable to human life, indeed that a life
> without friends was not really worth living.
>
> —Hannah Arendt, *Men in Dark Times*

"I can lose anything!" At nine, I bragged about my losses even though I was always punished for them. I remember the punishments, not the boasting. But pride in my losing streak featured in my mother's set pieces, whenever she recalled my character flaws, long after I had left home. I can imagine making the claim though, in a moment of bravado, standing up to her rage. Maybe it was a disclaimer: I can't help it; it's not about you, pushing past shame.

Did this history explain my panic on the disappearance of a pair of gold earrings a few summers ago in a little house we owned then near Stony Brook? One morning, just as I always did, I reached for the earrings on the bedside table where I had left them the night before, but they had vanished. I stood there, bewildered, fearful, expecting—what? A punishment that never came, nor did the earrings reappear.

Naturally, they were not any pair of earrings. They had been handmade by Resia Schor, my friend Naomi's mother, who was an artist and a jeweler. Sandy, my husband and a graduate school friend of Naomi's, had bought them for me as a birthday present at least thirty years earlier. The gift of the earrings marked a moment in my friendship with Naomi when our bond was new and the two of us were engaged in a phase of intense identification and competition, with each other, but also—this is harder to explain—*for* each other.

The earrings were shaped like the outline of a daisy with uneven edges that bore the maker's hand—thin, flat, and elegant, each gold flower perfectly covered the two asymmetrical sets of holes in my earlobes. I always traveled with this pair because they were easy to wear—with anything—and comfortable. I am wearing them in my last, expired, passport picture and in my author photo.

⊞ ⊞ ⊞

The losing score: one pair of earrings, three close friends: Carolyn Heilbrun, Naomi Schor, Diane Middlebrook.

From 2001 to 2007, nearly a decade of grief to open the new millennium.

⊞ ⊞ ⊞

The stories of these three life-changing friendships all bear the burden of loss. I cannot look back without feeling weighed down by their endings: suicide, cerebral hemorrhage, cancer. It's hard to resist mourning, and mostly I don't, but I want also to return to beginnings—the excitement of unfoldings—and, in retrospect, to remember how these friendships, two long-lasting, one brief but intense, shaped my emotional biography and the map of my brain. I could not have figured out who I was without them. Simply, not that it's ever simple, for starters, I'll say that each of these women made my life worth living because we believed in each other. I will cop to Hallmark card sentiment for now.

The shape of these stories has a lot to do with the luck of history, the passions of seventies feminism that challenged the academic world in which we all worked. But in the end, what mattered was how we grew into ourselves together with that luck. And how we lived our relationships had as much to do with the tapestry of our sometimes inchoate desires as our politics. Despite the rhetoric of sisterhood we embraced, a bond meant to transcend negative emotions, we suffered our share of envy and competitiveness, emotions a familiar part of the feminine palette we had inherited. The feelings were not always beautiful, and were hard to root out, but like so many other women, we came to view our friendships as a crucial piece in a new narrative.

Friends mourning their losses have offered the world most of the autobiographical accounts of friendship, and the most beautiful. Elegy is the preferred mode of friendship memorialization for men, Montaigne famously, but also for women. There's nothing like death to offer the kind of closure that allows for shapely storytelling. But elegy is also one sided. The survivor tells the story. Even if the letters and emails in my possession carry the voice of the missing friend, inevitably I am the editor, as well as the teller, for two, even if I want—and I do—to be a faithful reporter.

There's a certain solace in writing about loss, too, of course, because it's a way of coming to terms with mortality. As long as you are doing the writing, you are rehearsing the losing; unlike the friend, you are still there. You are the mourner, after all. But what happens when you start losing yourself? When, while fixed on the other, you discover that your position, secured among the living, is unstable, unsure? You may have imagined yourself safely on the side of the living, and then suddenly, like me, you are on the verge, possibly, of disappearing yourself. Not long after I began to write the stories of these friendships, I was diagnosed with advanced-stage lung cancer ("incurable but treatable," as my laconic oncologist put it when he delivered the prognosis). While I was struggling to understand what that might mean—how long would I live? how I would live?—I wanted to abandon this project. I had been writing from the place of the one who remained behind. Suddenly I was mourning myself.

I had been writing about the friends I missed; now I was forced to imagine that other friends would mourn me. Did that mean that I had joined the object position, and, if so, was the difference between us merely a matter of timing? Was that all? No, not yet. Split in two, I still wanted to be the subject; I wanted to be in charge of the story even if it seemed I had lost control of the narrative.

Cancer above all destroys the ordinary divisions of time through which we take for granted the capacity—however illusory—of severing past from present, present from future. To write about the friends I had lost in the past, while no longer believing that life in the present was propelling me, however slowly, into some kind of future, made me feel that I no longer had a place from which to write. Would there even be time to tell these stories?

But living with cancer in the twenty-first century, it turns out, does not necessarily mean the abrupt end of story, though it does, of course, mean worrying about how the story will end. It's a newish gift of modernity, something of a poisoned gift, but a gift nevertheless. I want to make the most of it, this strange situation, to add to the stock of friendship stories, since I know that in having made my life with friends, I have not been alone. If I've come to any wisdom about friendship, and it's as hard to say anything original about these bonds as it is about living with cancer, it's that without friends, part of us remains missing, the part that needs to look beyond our narrow boundaries to negotiate with what's not us. So here's the cancer trick I've learned: As long as I'm writing about my friends, I'm keeping them alive, and in keeping them alive, I'm staying alive with them. We are still in conversation, even if I'm doing most of the talking.

Carolyn Heilbrun

They will know that there are books waiting for them
as there were no books for me.

—Carolyn G. Heilbrun, *Women's Lives: The View from the Threshold*

1
Carolyn

CAROLYN, FEMINISM, AND ME

Then someone says yes to it.

—Gertrude Stein, *The Making of Americans*

Carolyn had just turned fifty. To Carolyn, fifty was a kind of watershed. The conventional marker of age meant, among other things, publicly declaring that she was old, growing her hair long enough to pull into a bun, and giving up on dresses. "Aging set me free," she went on to write. It became her great theme. And it was in the wake of turning fifty, when Carolyn made the decision to age, and to express that physically, that our friendship took root. I was thirty-five, feeling like a heroine who had lost the plot.

At one of our early lunches at Au Grenier, a restaurant one flight up at Broadway and 113th Street, Carolyn announced that she was inaugurating the aging process by giving in to gaining weight. "The hell with living on celery," she said, looking skeptically at my salad.

By dessert she had offered me a dusty rose-colored ultra-suede suit with a belted jacket and a straight, below-the-knee skirt she could no longer wear. Fortunately, the suit didn't fit me since I was much too intimidated by Carolyn then to say, "Pink ultra-suede? Moi?"

▣ ▣ ▣

We had met in 1976 at Columbia as members of the newly created Mellon Society of Fellows—I was the junior fellow to her senior. (Columbia will be a character in our story, leading man and villain.) Team teaching was part of the two-year Mellon mandate, pairing a senior faculty member with a junior one. When Carolyn proposed that we teach a graduate course together, I was both thrilled and terrified.

In 1976, Carolyn was a powerful force on the Columbia campus, one of the very few tenured women and a well-known figure in the English department, filled with strong, equally well-known, intellectual convictions. I was an insecure assistant professor of French, flailing, failing in my life, anxious about tenure. Carolyn had served on the committee to select the junior people for the fellowship (as had my dissertation advisor, Michael Riffaterre) and told me not long after our introduction that she had picked me, insisted on me, because I was a feminist. I've never been completely sure why, beyond wanting a feminist colleague, she then took me up as she did, in an almost Jamesian way. But I'm glad she did, since I would not have made the first step, and we'd never have become friends.

I did not understand then how embattled Carolyn felt, despite her position.

What I saw was a woman not remotely like me: with tenure and books (including several detective novels published under a pseudonym), a woman with a nice husband, three children, and an apartment on Central Park West. What I admired, it turns out, was part of what made her resented by many in the department. Early that fall, a youngish, rather successful male colleague of Carolyn in the English department, whom I had known in graduate school, warned me, when I told him about our future team teaching, "Stay away from Carolyn Heilbrun. She's a bitch." I had trouble squaring his portrait, which he would not explain ("You'll see"), with the woman I already admired and found generous and kind. His comment made me nervous, though, but not enough to reject the opportunity to know her. Much later I learned that his view of Carolyn prevailed widely in the department, no doubt in somewhat more polite language among the old establishment fogeys, who said she wasn't "collegial."

Carolyn liked to picture our relationship as a study in contrasts. In 1994, in her foreword to a British collection of essays about women and aging (notably menopause), she painted the two of us through sartorial metaphors:

> I will wager that two friends with more diverse views on aging and menopause than Nancy and I have would be hard to find. But then we are friends readily distinguishable on many grounds. I, for example, am often asked how I can bear to endure constant intimacy with someone who always looks so fastidiously groomed. This question, asked in the face of my own apparel, suggestive of one who has just returned from herding sheep, ought to be reversed: how can she, so very French in her put-togetherness from hairstyle to shoes, bear to confront, as she weekly does, my rumpledness?

Even though I was, at least when we first met, the structuralist critic, Carolyn was also enamored of the very center of structuralist theory: the binary opposition. The attraction of our friendship, as she saw it, depended on how dissimilar we were. Although Naomi and I often dwelled on how we were different, we also saw ourselves as alike. We fluctuated between those two poles, but, especially at the beginning, what we had in common trumped all: our writing, our inferior status at Columbia, our anxiety about the future, our wildly unsatisfactory relations with men. The differences between Carolyn and me were of another order. For one thing, whereas Carolyn was embracing aging, I was dreading it.

Naturally, Carolyn never looked as if she had just returned from herding sheep, though the conceit is a measure of her style of self-deprecation (in fact, she always dressed rather neatly), and I looked French only in her eyes. For one thing, my kinky hair alone would have disqualified me, no matter how expensive the cut. But Carolyn enjoyed posing our personas as polar opposites, English and French tastes for starters, hence the implausibility—and value—of our bond. How could we possibly be friends given our disparate appearances?

There was, as Carolyn explained in her foreword, "feminism, humanism, a passion for reading and writing, and, because of our very dissimilarities, the chance to cheer each other over the fences that stall our purposeful journeys and our idle rambles." It's true, and yet I find myself stalled—to pick up her verb—when faced with this rosy summary. Feminism allowed us to share part of our academic journeys despite, or perhaps because of, as she says, our dissimilarities, and to see each other through, but it was also her story.

Certainly, as she recognized, when young, we would not have been tempted to become friends; even in 1976, even with feminism, the disparity in our situations and histories was impossible to ignore. Later in the foreword Carolyn reiterates her confidence in the power of aging to overcome those differences: "The answer," she maintains, "is that such things no longer matter to friends such as we; friendships with women are perhaps the choicest rewards of aging." Did such things continue to matter for us?

For Carolyn, friendship trumped all.

For Carolyn, first we were friends, then friends with differences.

Friendship between women, along with the advantages of age, were two of the great subjects lodged at the heart of Carolyn's lifelong project to reinterpret and revalue women's lives, a kind of grand, collective biography. In describing the two of us, for example, she combined the themes in this reflection about our differences and how, contrary to appearances, in the end they didn't matter:

> I have three children, she has none, and were we youthful, we might regard each other's state with more envy than accord. Our parental condition today, on the other hand, is remarkably similar; I delight in my grown children, Nancy in the young women she has mentored with a devotion and affection greater, I have no doubt, than that possible to their natural mothers. (Motherhood carries such an emotional wallop that to be an adult mother is to be either intelligently disengaged, though interested, or unhappily bereft of filial attentions.)

Is being a mother of adult children "remarkably similar" to being a mentor to graduate students? Carolyn liked to think so but

I never did. There is nothing more crucial to who I am than the fact of my not having had children, without, however, being someone who hadn't ever wanted them in the first place. That would have been easy. I did not not want children, I just waited too long to want them—age, not the version Carolyn was celebrating, worked against me. Carolyn lived through the dismal years of my infertility drama in the early 1980s with compassion in the face of repeated failures, so I see in this quasi equivalency between mothering and mentoring an expression of her wish, a decade later, to close the gap between us at any cost, as if repressing the difference could erase my sense of loss. I think now the collapse of the two roles was meant as a consolation prize of sorts.

Still. "She has none." Carolyn's optimism notwithstanding, I certainly envied the corresponding fact of her three children then. (Envy has always been my fallback emotion, despite persistent efforts to root it out, and Carolyn's belief that we had aged past the envy stage in friendship was more hopeful than true. But even for me, posthumous envy is a bridge too far.) More to the point, perhaps, about what the differences between us meant to our bond from Carolyn's perspective is her not factoring into the equation her own role as mentor, a role she performed masterfully, and for which not only I but also generations of younger women were grateful. I know she felt she had written a heroic number of letters of recommendation for all of us though I do not recall her ever using the word *mentor* about herself, and she never used it in relation to me.

Nonetheless, long after the fact, when I read *Sir Vidia's Shadow*, Paul Theroux's memoir of his friendship with V. S. Naipaul, I saw clearly how that aspect of the age difference plays itself out. In the memoir, for example, Theroux describes meeting the writer as a young man just starting out. Naipaul was ten years older: "He had believed in me. He had talked about how in writing you served an apprenticeship." "Books make their way," Carolyn liked to say in consolation for the abyss into which one of my books had fallen. "You'll see, it's early days." For Theroux (sounding like Carolyn on the meaning of friendship), "Friendship is plainer but deeper than love. A friend knows your faults and forgives them." (She did, even my dislike of dogs.) "But more than that a friend is a witness. I needed Vidia as a friend, because he saw something in me I did not see. He said I was a writer," wrote Theroux. This Carolyn also said, and I needed to hear.

I'm not suggesting that the volatile, unequal relationship between the two macho writers was a model for friendship anyone would wish to emulate (least of all Carolyn), especially since their story did not turn out well. (After thirty years of friendship, Vidia dumped Paul.) But I'm keeping the idea of friend as witness. Like Naipaul, Carolyn was already a writer, "The Writer," when we met. I had barely begun. And just as Naipaul did for Theroux, she made something happen, by seeing what I did not see in myself.

Witness was further complicated in our case by the fact that the two of us came into relation within an academic institution narrowed by hierarchy, not the wide world of literature in which the two novelists roamed. At Columbia, Carolyn acted not only as witness—believing in me as a writer—but also as protector within our violent little universe on the shores of the Hudson.

Of course, it's not hard to notice what any woman would: Where is the reciprocity in acts of witness like these? Carolyn believed in, felt, reciprocity between us, and she inscribed it in every book she signed. It's much harder for me to see what, in turn, I bore witness to in my view of her; what, bluntly, I did in return.

What Carolyn did for me, was for me, I could never be, do for her.

She saved my life; I did not save hers.

That haunts me.

DINNERS WITH CAROLYN

Once a week, for a little over twenty years, Carolyn and I would have dinner together on the Upper West Side. For the first ten years, beginning at the tail end of the 1970s, we lived in walking distance of each other, I on the northeast corner of truck-trafficked Amsterdam Avenue, Carolyn facing the tree line of Central Park West. Well into the 1980s, there still were neighborhood restaurants where the atmosphere was unprepossessing, the food unremarkable, and the noise level—not measured at the time (this was before shouting across the table had become a regular feature of communication)—a steady background murmur. The food mattered less to Carolyn than the fact of being out to eat, not in someone's home, not with family. "The conversation's the thing," she would say. "It doesn't matter what you eat." Although she acknowledged there were limits to how bad the food could be before it became unacceptable, even washed down with significant amounts of alcohol. This was so-called American food before nouvelle cuisine brought dishes laden with ingredients the waiters had to name in addition to themselves, and before all the elements of the meal arrived stacked vertically in minuscule portions. It was also before Zagat and Yelp ratings had become de rigueur. Each time you tried a new restaurant, you were on your own.

Two women having dinner on their own and talking over wine: That was Carolyn's ideal of female friendship, Woolf's Chloe and Olivia in their laboratory. And once we had begun teaching together, and created the Gender and Culture series at Columbia University Press, in the early eighties, we reckoned that we were doing business, and that our dinners were, in theory at least, tax deductible—a laboratory of our own.

Until email took hold in the late 1990s, we rarely connected between dinners. I have a few letters from summer separations, by far Carolyn's wittiest exercises in style, and the vehicle for her most endearing persona. We almost never spoke on the phone. As a result, at dinner there was everything to report on, from books, to school, to husbands and moods. The agenda typically included a dose of complaints, usually by me about my life, but sometimes by Carolyn, especially about Columbia. I often felt that I provided a kind of entertainment, especially when I was miserable. It's not that she was cruel; on the contrary. But in the distribution of roles between us, I was the wretched one dealing with life crises—tenure, infertility, depression—she the rock. I could not help narrating my misery with a kind of stand-up, antic energy, and she enjoyed it from the audience.

At first, we ate at Dobson's, a Columbus Avenue staple that closed when the neighborhood gentrified. The regular menu offered half a roast chicken along with mashed potatoes and salad. Carolyn, who had no time for nonsense, always ordered the chicken rather than spending her energy analyzing the menu, which never changed. But when placing her order, another side of her would come out. Preferring the dark meat and not wishing to leave the choice to chance, she would look up and ask in a timid, flirty, little-girl voice whether she could please have what she called, after a tiny pause, the bottom. The waiters routinely, gallantly acquiesced to her request, but I was astounded by the emergence of that deferential little voice from a woman who typically commanded a great deal of authority, who intimidated strangers, students, and occasionally, me. The only other time she used that voice, or a variation of its upward tones, was with dogs.

After a while, even Carolyn tired of Dobson's and roast chicken, so for a while we met at my apartment, ordering takeout from Saigon Grill, the popular Vietnamese restaurant that had to shut down when scandal revealed that the owners had been paying their workers below minimum wage, sometimes less than two dollars an hour. But she didn't like having to wait to be announced by the doorman and then wait for the slow elevator, always busy at the dinner hour, followed by waiting for the Broadway bus home, so the arrangement did not last long. Finally, we settled on Akaihana, a quiet Japanese restaurant, almost around the corner from her home, which disappeared sometime in the early 2000s, replaced by more boisterous venues. The menu at Akaihana was reliable, if unexciting, and though the waiters clearly found us comical— an odd couple (not mother and daughter, but what? Colleagues, we reassured them)—they saved our preferred table. (Mind you, we were hardly the only strange-appearing people among the regulars; notably, there was also a very thin man dressed in a running outfit, with long, dyed carrot-colored hair, tied in a low ponytail, who always ate alone.) Carolyn took a dim view of raw fish, but she finally accepted a weekly dose of sashimi, though she insisted on a fork for the rice.

TEACHING WITH CAROLYN

I was lying in bed leafing through the *New Yorker* when my eye was caught by the opening line of a story: "It was easy to find an apartment in New Haven, even though my classes in feminist criticism were starting in just a few days and most of the other grad students had arrived at Yale the week before." I was riveted.

"Engagements" was a story by a woman writer about feminist criticism in the stylish setting of the *New Yorker*. It was 1985.

Feminist criticism disappears until well into the third page, when the narrator, a young woman named Cora, mentions that she had been accepted into the Women's Studies Program at Yale. At the time, I was directing the Women's Studies Program at Barnard, teaching feminist criticism at Columbia, and more than mildly curious about where the story was going. "I was sitting in class, taking notes as usual," Cora reports, "when it became apparent that not one word that was being said made the slightest bit of sense." Curiosity segued into anxiety.

"The teacher, Anna Castleton" (I wondered who she was), a "well-padded, grayish woman with clipped-poodle hair" (that's not Margaret Homans, the one feminist professor in the Yale English department I could think of), "was discussing a conference she had attended the week before—a Poetics of Gender colloquium—where she was severely attacked for her presentation." Not Margaret, then. In fact, the poodle-haired professor was starting to sound a lot like me. But wait, I resisted, this doesn't make sense. I had organized the Poetics of Gender conference at Columbia the previous fall. And I hadn't been attacked there.

Still, when Cora quoted from her notes, I quickly recognized the drift of things I had said in class about a feminist conference at Brown the previous spring at which I had given a talk about female authorship in the wake of the "death of the author" concept that we academic types believed in at the time. I called it "Changing the Subject," taking as my example Charlotte Brontë's feisty feminist heroine, Lucy Snowe. A young British theorist in the audience had stood up and read a statement denouncing my talk. This exchange was recast by Cora in her seminar notes:

> Status of empirical discourse.
> Post-structuralist account of dissolving subject precludes for-mation of female identity.
> The notion of the subject in progress.
> It was assumed that she was calling for a return to fixed identity.
> Post-gendered subjectivities.
> If gender is constructed, a gendered identity 99 percent of the time is built onto a person who has a sex.

"Without using 'class,' she argued for a more complicated view of women as historical subject. Yet she was attacked for this—brutally attacked," Cora wrote. Carolyn and I were teaching a course on heroines in French and English novels that year. I doubt that we spent the two hours of the seminar revisiting the event, especially since Carolyn eschewed all jargon, including the feminist kind. But we had become fused into a single feminist professor, well padded and gray haired, as we both were; we had become "Anna Castleton."

Despite the somewhat garbled version of what I had said—not, of course, that I remembered exactly what I had said—Cora had gotten the gist of my account, delivered in class the week after the conference as I struggled to absorb the shock of public censure.

I had to admire the clever recasting of my narrative in the story, even if through her distortions, the young woman neatly skewered the professor, who, at this point, was clearly enough me: "I wondered whether the teacher had burst into tears following the attack on her. The two hours of class were devoted to a retelling of the attack, couched in this language which so gracefully circled a subject without ever landing to make a point."

Recalling the scene as I read in bed, newly mortified, I did feel like crying. The writer was taking no hostages. I poured myself another glass of bourbon.

But the story wasn't over. Once I (likened in Cora's notebook doodle to a "beaver, paddling frantically, with a tree stump clutched in its large buck teeth") had been dispatched with utter ridicule, Cora turned the spotlight on herself, describing a presentation she had made in the same seminar later in the semester, on themes of mysticism and Eastern philosophy in the writings of Virginia Woolf. I remembered the moment quite vividly, but it was no longer Tama Janowitz, the story's author, whom I had begun to visualize in her place around the seminar table, but her fictional friend Cora; they always sat together.

The presentation had not gone well. "I had hoped to please the teacher," Cora confesses, but "when I finished, she looked up and said, 'You're wrong.'" The other women in the class all turned to catch my reaction. I felt as if I had been electrocuted on a television game show."

Carolyn was a well-known critic and Woolf scholar whose writings the real-life Cora had clearly not read. I waited nervously, in silence, as Carolyn explained her response. "You're wrong" had not been delivered in anger. She said it calmly, though without compassion for the student, and the words reverberated around the seminar table on the sixth floor of Philosophy Hall, in a wood-paneled room hung with the portraits of famous dead male professors of English. She had said it differently from the way, on the fifth floor of Philosophy Hall, my famously cruel dissertation advisor used to interrupt after only a few words of a student presentation, but the effect was the same. "No," he would say, glaring at the petrified student, cutting her off mid-sentence. Like Virginia Woolf's Professor von X in *A Room of One's Own*, Riffaterre radiated anger.

How, you may ask, can I even put the feminist and the patriarch, my warring mentors, together in the same paragraph? Her "wrong," his "no"? In his dismissal, the patriarch typically took the opportunity to reiterate his theory of the literary text (which we all were meant to know and rehearse). Carolyn, a well-known authority on Woolf's writing, offered a less autobiographical, more generic, second-wave feminist argument. The student, she explained, "had fallen prey to a traditional male put-down: placing women in the category of weak, dreamy mystics and thus denying them power." Cora concludes that Castleton only wants to hear that line of thought. Soon after this episode, she gave up on graduate school and returned to live in New York.

I called Carolyn at her country house in the Berkshires, even though it was quite late. She had not seen the story and was sure I was overreacting. After all, her comments were meant to be instructive. Her intent was to help the young woman understand the presuppositions that had led her to an erroneous view of Woolf. If the student was devastated by what she perceived to be an unfair exertion of authority, well, she was insufficiently tough minded. Besides, it was just a story, a *New Yorker* story at that—fiction. No one would think it was about us.

I prayed she was right: that no one I knew would see the story and guess it was about Carolyn and me and not a dowdy, overbearing professor at Yale. I still don't know whether anyone did; at any rate, it never was mentioned. Rereading the story now, some thirty years later, what surprises me is how little feminist criticism—or, as it's referred to in the *New Yorker*'s online abstract, "feminine criticism"—had to do with the story's arc, which turned on the heroine's decision not to marry a strange, slacker guy—hence the title "Engagements." After the disappointing semester at "Yale," Cora temporarily lives with her mother, as she tries to figure out her future. Carolyn and I were just filler.

I don't think I knew who Tama Janowitz was in 1985, though I did when she republished "Engagements" in *Slaves of New York* a few years later, a collection that brought her a measure of celebrity. Mean as the story felt to me, humiliating, really, I could not completely dismiss its representation of Carolyn's and my teaching. As I already had learned, feminists could be cruel to each other in public: I had taken that body blow at the Brown conference, and Cora had felt that at "Yale." Janowitz defended her friend with the tool of her trade: fiction. Maybe it all evened out.

Still, aren't there times when "you're wrong" is what needs saying, even between women? I sometimes think that what feels intolerable—like electrocution—is the slippage from the power of the woman professor to the memory of the critical mother so many of us endured growing up, the woman we don't want to be.

Mixed in with my Carolyn files, I found a typewritten document from September 1977, a kind of diary page, in which I record the first meeting of a new course, "French Women Writers: Toward a Definition of a Feminine Text." I confess my guilt about teaching, not to mention launching the course—the first ever offered on women writers in the French department at Columbia—on Rosh Hashanah.

I felt the whole time that I was in a trance: Time went by so quickly. After the class, Louise came over and kissed me on the cheek. Alice said bravo. It was incredibly moving. To have done it. To have decided to do it and then see it happen. I know I will have to work very hard. But I want to.

Difficulty too, with authority: to tell Sandra she was "wrong"... and she was. Who am I to say? I still feel like a student. What do *I* know?

It is always strange to come across lines you no longer remember writing, even when you remember the experience it records. It's hard to know what you are like, who you are, when you are the teacher, and particularly when early in your career, you are teaching graduate students not much younger than you.

I also found in those files a letter from Carolyn, dated just before Thanksgiving of that same semester, with an edit of the description for the course we were planning to co-teach the following spring: "Your paragraph was fine: I have pared it down a bit. Let me know what you think." Carolyn told me early on that her motto for successful writing was one she had adopted from Marianne Moore: to write in a language that "cats and dogs" could read. My course description was slightly different:

> The heroine's text, the trajectory of a female destiny, is at the heart of the novel in the French and English tradition. We will read, in a historical perspective, novels by male and female authors. Drawing upon recent investigations in several disciplines, we will

attempt to identify the intrapsychic, cultural and literary phenomena that govern the process by which major female characters are inscribed.

Oy. Not yet ready for cats and dogs. We taught the course the following spring, and it unlocked a new phase in my writing, rousing me from my paralysis: I finally revised the dissertation for publication two years later, borrowing our course title, *The Heroine's Text*.

In November 1977, Carolyn and I were still on formal terms—she signed the letter "yours" (I don't remember exactly when "love" came in).

Not friends yet.

I'LL BE YOUR MIRROR

When we want to see ourselves, Aristotle famously suggested, we have only to look in a mirror. In the same way, when we want to *know* ourselves, we look at our friend's face, since the "friend is, as we assert, a second self." Of course, in fourth-century BC Athens, the bonds of friendship meant a relationship among citizens belonging to a certain social rank and history, which, with rare exceptions, did not include women (nor, naturally, did the model apply to slaves). Cicero continues the conceit. "When a man thinks of a true friend," he writes in "On Friendship," "he is looking at himself in the mirror." A "real friend" is "as it were, another self." So why bother about Aristotle or Cicero today?

Like Aristotle, we moderns, too, like to think of friendship as an extraordinary good, a life-enhancing relationship between two equals. How might his reflection model for friendship's ability to create self-knowledge work for women? Mirrors, we know from fairy tales, can be devastating (mirror, mirror on the wall). For example, what if, as is true for many women, the face I see in the mirror is not a face I especially like? Suppose what I'm seeing is the face composed by my mother's critical gaze? But then, suppose my new friend reflects not the portrait I inherited, but an entirely other, different self, a self I had not imagined? What I love about such a friend is precisely her capacity to see another face, different from the one I know.

That's the self I want to inhabit: *that* second self.

For as long as I can remember, I've only ever wanted to be someone else.

⊞ ⊞ ⊞

Probably the most beautiful line about friendship in his essay "Of Friendship" is Montaigne's explanation of why he loved the friend lost to him, the famous "because" of ineffability: "Because it was he, because it was I." The two first met as writers at a "gathering in the city" and were so immediately "taken with each other" that they both felt theirs would be a bond for life. The loss came only four years later. "I was already so formed and accustomed to being a second self everywhere," Montaigne writes, "that only half of me seems to be alive now."

Although our most important friendships may not attain quite the emotional pitch dramatized in Montaigne's essay, of course, we continue to value the place of friendships in our lives. In his recent study *On Friendship*, the philosopher Alexander Nehamas raises questions about feelings that did not fit the Greek model of *philia*, perfect friendship between virtuous men. He describes what he calls friendship's "double face," noting that "even the best of friendships sometimes conflict with the morally right thing to do." Because friendship can also bring "dangers and disappointments," he writes, these disappointments "may actually be the other face" of friendship's "pleasures and benefits."

Nehamas draws his examples from the bonds between men. The sole relationship between women he takes up with any detail is that between the two protagonists in *Thelma and Louise*. The 1991 film comes to illustrate his point about the imbricated ways in which "friendship and immorality" can be entwined. It's true, of course, that Thelma and Louise encounter disaster on their road trip and that shooting and robbing aren't the most honorable activities for any pair seeking adventure (nobody's perfect). Still, many women loved the movie when it came out because we are starved for examples of women taking center stage.

Despite Nehamas's lack of interest in what friendship between women might look like, I borrow the coinage of "double face." But I'm also recasting the metaphor slightly to describe the nature of intimate ties between women as "double-sided," having, like records from another era, an A-side and a B-side. Double-sidedness maintains the intrinsic twoness of the friendship model while avoiding linguistic contamination from its nasty neighbor "two-faced." While the B-side is often neglected by listeners, it is nonetheless inseparable from the spectacular appeal of the A-side. The B-side in a relationship story, I'm suggesting, may include the less beautiful emotions that sometimes haunt friendships, even if we tend to overlook their power, enamored as we are of A-side's hit tunes. But why limit ourselves to the binary? Friendship is more complicated than that, including the possibility of needing both sides at once.

TALKING, WALKING, DOGS, AND DETECTIVES

The "untold story of friendship between women," Carolyn believed, was key to uncovering the emotional patterns in women's lives that biographers tend to miss. In *Writing a Woman's Life*, she celebrates the intense ties between Vera Brittain and Winifred Holtby, two British women writers, whose relationship she describes as "a constant and continuous dialogue that only death could halt." In looking for models to help excavate the layers of my friendships, Brittain and Holtby, admirable as they were, felt too remote (they met after World War I), too English to be useful, even while the notion of an uninterrupted dialogue felt true, especially since that's mainly all I ever do in my friendships: talk. But I found a path back to Carolyn, at least partway back, in a more recent example of two women attached to their dialogue in Gail Caldwell's poignant memoir of her friendship with Caroline Knapp, *Let's Take the Long Way Home*. My stories did not have much in common with theirs, in the details, but I was seduced by the language of their emotions, which I found not just compelling, but uncannily familiar.

The memoir opens this way: "It's an old, old story: I had a friend and we shared everything, and then she died and so we shared that, too." That seemed a good beginning for a story of friendship between women that in fact was not old in the telling, a story of grief.

I wondered, immediately captured, what kinds of things did they share?

For Gail and Caroline, what's shared is a passion first for dogs (training them), doubled by another passion—originally Caroline's alone, then acquired by Gail, under her friend's tutelage—for rowing, which together give the book's world its particularity and its palpable joy. The title points to a wish for more time: "Let's take the long way home," Caroline would say, as the two prepared to separate after a long walk with their dogs, a desire, a need, to keep the conversation going.

Now as a reader, hungry for a story of friendship between women as a way of assuaging my loss of women friends, I had, I confess, to make a significant detour around the dogs and the bodies of water—skipping big chunks of narrative, while I remained ashore, relentlessly urban and petless. But since I identified with the emotion threaded through the story, I followed along, guided by the pleasure of finding myself a lazy spectator of the women's exertions.

The constant presence of the adored creatures, though, gave me the occasion to ponder Carolyn's love of dogs and my bewilderment, irritation, or boredom when faced with anyone's animal worship, especially hers, which extended to whatever urban dog one was likely to come across when we strolled home after our weekly dinners on Broadway. Growing up on the Upper West Side of Manhattan, walking to and from school, I crisscrossed the streets, sometimes dodging traffic, to avoid encountering a dog head on. Given the number of neighborhood specimens, I invariably ended up late for school or late home from school for lunch. I had inherited this fear from my father, who seemed ill at ease with any kind of animal and in fact inadvertently killed my goldfish one summer when I was away at camp by feeding them matzo instead of fish food.

But I was thrilled to read a memoir centered on a friendship between women, even if I had to skirt the dogs. I was pulled in by the love between them; even more so, I envied them for it.

I don't know about the rowing parts, but Carolyn would have been entranced by Caldwell's narrative: two women who could not stop talking to each other, especially about their dogs. Her attraction to dogs was irresistible, and she would stop to engage with whatever species we crossed (she recognized every breed) in a tone of voice she reserved for animals and restaurant waiters, a kind of lilting uncertainty. She was also known to schmooze with horses, when the opportunity arose, often in Central Park. She believed she could communicate with animals, and maybe she did.

Carolyn described her love for dogs, and in particular, Bianca, whom she adopted in late life and to whom she devoted a chapter in her essay collection *The Last Gift of Time*, as an essential form of emotional sustenance: "I experienced my need for canine companionship suddenly, as a compulsion, a necessity of my sixties." A dog in New York meant that she'd have to leave the house to walk the dog, and hence herself, since she was tempted by reclusion: A "dog was required to turn stability into action." Bianca, a rescue dog from the Humane Society, adored Carolyn with a single and singular attachment, following her from room to room in the apartment, dogging, I want to say, her footsteps.

In early June 2000, three years after Carolyn published "The Dog Who Came to Stay" and three years before her suicide, Bianca died. Carolyn wrote to her friend and biographer, Susan Kress, describing the extreme sorrow she felt at the loss of the dog. And then, as always, she found an apposite literary quotation, this time from Kipling's lines about dogs and heartbreak. Carolyn was well aware of the danger that might come from giving her heart to a dog: "Of course there is always a price. But the fear of paying it, I convinced myself before giving in to my need for a dog, is the highest price of all." I learned of Bianca's death after the ritual end of one of our Japanese dinners, when Carolyn, finishing her green tea, said gnomically that she had something she needed to tell me. We walked the few blocks to the Eleanor Roosevelt statue at 72nd Street in Riverside Park, a place we occasionally went for important conversations. When we reached the statue, Carolyn told me what had happened. She didn't weep, but her face went pale, as it often did when she was affected by a strong emotion.

I don't believe she expected me to say anything appropriate or even helpful. She wanted me to know she was suffering, a rare avowal. The only time people mourn unambivalently, she said as I walked her home, is for an animal. I believed her, as I tended to believe her statements about how the world works, especially about children, men, and marriage, and I knew she was sharing a suffering not matched by her words. She thought she had been willing to pay the price of choosing attachment. But anticipating grief and being knocked into it are never quite the same thing.

"The heart breaks open," Caldwell quotes a friend saying, meeting her soon after the death of her beloved dog, Clemmie. "I know now," she writes in response to the comment, "that we never get over great losses; we absorb them, and they carve us into different, often kinder, creatures." Carolyn went on to get another dog, as Gail did, but the memoir ends before we know how she will be changed by her losses.

"Caroline's death was a vacancy in the heart," Caldwell writes. "I knew I would never have another friend like Caroline." Friendships don't repeat.

⊞ ⊞ ⊞

Later that same year, at a dinner in November 2000 just before Thanksgiving, Carolyn reached across the table and handed me her thirteenth and penultimate mystery, *Honest Doubt*. Early on, the story features a dog integrated into a kind of self-portrait by the narrator. This first-person narrator, known by the nickname "Woody," is a P.I. who enlists Kate Fansler—Carolyn's gorgeous amateur sleuth and star of many of the Amanda Cross novels—for help in an investigation into the death of a professor of English literature, a Tennyson specialist. The setting is a college campus peopled by characters familiar to Amanda Cross readers, including many unsavory, aggressively misogynistic types. (It's neither hard nor entirely far-fetched to imagine Carolyn still reliving the years at Columbia during which she could never make the story turn out well for her or her young colleagues.)

The book opens with Woody's self-presentation as a fat woman detective, set in juxtaposition to the enviably slender Kate on the second page: "I, being fat, dislike thin women. . . ." In a moment of largesse, however, Woody decides Kate might be a good partner, despite her lithe silhouette. A disquisition on the meaning of fat continues, almost relentlessly: "I collect plump people who are accomplished as well as heavy. It helps to knit up my raveled self-esteem." Dorothy Sayers, Carolyn's heroine in the world of detective stories, she adds, "was fat." The detective's monologue stays on point: "I'm afraid I've gotten in the habit of mentioning my size to bring it out into the open," so that it won't stand in the way of forming a connection. Choosing an androgynous name like Woody, she explains, was motivated by the same anxiety, the desire to bracket the fatness "so people wouldn't know I was a woman until they were face-to-face with me. Right, I thought, they wouldn't know I was fat, either." Neither a woman, nor a fat woman.

Many of the themes about self-presentation in *Honest Doubt* echo earlier versions in *The Last Gift of Time*, especially the essay

"On Not Wearing Dresses." Carolyn describes there the grand renunciation after the "mid-body expansion" of her mid-fifties, a comedy of errors, leading her loyal husband to wonder whether in one of her experiments with plus sizes, she was wearing a tent: "What was soon obvious was that in dresses I resembled a walking bolster; in my pants and tunic, I was noticeably less bolsterish." The creation of the new style includes a reassertion of earlier arguments about androgyny and identity: Androgyny, she felt, had the potential to "free individuals from the prison of gender," and it gave her continued pleasure to assume the garb of her "androgynous self." (Her controversial *Toward a Recognition of Androgyny* had appeared in 1973, more than twenty years earlier.)

At a conference panel devoted to Carolyn's contributions to Woolf scholarship, held in London in 2004, Victoria Rosner, who had organized the panel, read from an exchange of letters between Morris Beja, a well-known modernist, and Carolyn. Beja described how, in 1975, he tried to persuade Carolyn to accept the post of president of what came to be called the International Virginia Woolf Society by promising to do all the time-consuming work if only she would lend her name. Carolyn resisted on various grounds: "Should I," she wondered, "like Virginia Woolf at another occasion simply say I have nothing to wear?" To make the offer more appealing, Beja added how important all involved felt that the first president not be a man. When Carolyn finally accepted and gave the inaugural lecture in the fall of 1978, she noted that she had been asked to be the first president because she "was a woman." She went on to say that she wasn't a woman: "I'm androgynous."

When Carolyn fought on behalf of women, it wasn't necessarily because she saw herself as one. What she saw herself as was a feminist.

Carolyn was never as fat as she makes Woody out to be, though her clothes—the tunics and pants reminiscent of her fellow Wellesley alumna Hillary Clinton's famous pantsuits—made the shape of her body a mystery. I don't know where Hillary stands on dogs, big or small.

In *Honest Doubt*, a Saint Bernard makes an early cameo, leading to Woody's confession of being a canine lover: "I've got to admit I'm a nut about dogs." Woody greets Kate's dog ("Banny" after Anne Bancroft), and when she approaches, Woody recalls, "I put my hands around that great big head and cooed; well, that's what I did, I cooed, calling him a magnificent and beautiful creature." Ah, *cooing* was indeed the word I had been hunting for to describe Carolyn's manner of discourse with dogs, a tone strangely close to baby talk. "To a non-dog lover I would have sounded giddy, if not of questionable sanity," Woody says. But what's more surprising is not so much her love for the dog, but the way the dog and fat come together later in the chapter, as Woody takes her leave:

> I walked over to say goodbye to Banny . . . I thought to myself, She's big like a fat person; it's work to get up and easier to be agreeable from a reclining position. Besides, when you're big you have a sense of being in charge, no matter what is likely to occur. That was clearly how Banny felt, and I decided to feel that way too.

The self-portrait as a fat woman did not surprise me. Carolyn and I often talked both about her love for dogs and her views on being fat—why it mattered, why it shouldn't matter, why she cared, and why, she insisted, she didn't care. But I had never before heard her connect the dots between big woman and big dog.

(Caldwell relates an encounter with a wheelchair-bound elderly woman who wants to visit her dog Clemmie. "I like a *big* dog," the woman says, remembering dogs she had loved in the past. "I like a big dog, too," Caldwell says.)

What can I say? I was disturbed by Carolyn's portrait of the fat detective. It sounded like an obsession, I told her. Carolyn insisted that the portrait had nothing to do with her and was in fact inspired by Mary Thom, a well-known feminist *Ms.* editor who was heavy, and who, like the character Woody, rode a motorcycle. The cover showed a woman cyclist, speeding away into the darkness. Yes, she was on a "crusade," as Woody puts it later in the novel, but it was an impersonal, feminist defense.

Carolyn accused me of having forgotten how to read. Wasn't I the one who went on about the death of the author? Hadn't I heard of the creative process?

⊞ ⊞ ⊞

The following year, we made another journey to the Eleanor Roosevelt statue. It was early fall, still hot, too hot for Carolyn. She told me that when she was forty, while her children were young, she had undergone a radical mastectomy. She thought—everyone thought—that she was going to die. We had discussed many intimate, bodily things in detail, and yet she had remained silent about this mutilation. She explained that wearing a prosthesis was uncomfortable, that it was something of a production to put it on, and at the very least required preparation before leaving the house. It's not hard to connect the injury to the body to the desire for the fluidity of androgynous style—the freedom of not showing. Reading *Honest Doubt* now, I think how difficult Carolyn's body must have already felt to her when she settled in to the physical changes of her fifties, which then required another layer of camouflage. Had I known this piece of her history, I might have understood the self-portrait differently: as a way of asserting authority, taking charge, wanting comfort in her body.

I don't know why Carolyn told me about the cancer then, more than twenty years into our friendship. Perhaps because she knew we were nearing the end of our dialogue.

We have become accustomed to hearing about breast cancer ever since Betty Ford broke the silence in 1974. It does not seem strange to me that Carolyn would not have been public about the surgery in 1965. It does seem strange, though, that I learned about it in 2001, and also that in all the writing she did about women and their bodies and the need for women to break the silence, this was not a silence she would break.

We can try to know our friends, but sometimes we are destined to miss their most important truths.

AMBIGUOUS WOMEN: *WRITING A WOMAN'S LIFE*

Carolyn only once showed me work in manuscript: *Writing a Woman's Life*, arguably her most successful book of criticism. The inscription to me is dated September 8, 1988. She must have given me the pages the previous year, stopping by my apartment on our way to dinner; pub dates are always confusing. "You'll tell me what you think," she said, handing me the slender manuscript. "It's very short, and it's not Julia Kristeva." True, but it was Carolyn G. Heilbrun. She was sixty-two; I was forty-seven. Perhaps because the book had not only been dedicated to me, but also began with an epigraph from one of my essays about women's life writing, from the first I had no critical distance on the argument. Returning to the book now, and to our friendship in memory, I find myself reacting the way I always did with the Amanda Cross mysteries: like a detective looking for clues. What was the Carolyn story behind the Carolyn story she tells here, what she liked to call, with scare quotes, a subtext?

▣ ▣ ▣

The first words of the introduction set the tone for the kind of reach academics in the main both resist and admire: "There are four ways to write a woman's life." Right there you have classic, not to say vintage, Carolyn: the clarity, the confidence, the daring, the provocation. Four? Not three? Not five? That's part of why the book sold, at one point, one hundred fifty thousand copies and was reissued in paperback in 2008, twenty years later, with a preface by Katha Pollitt. Nothing in my training would have allowed me to make a statement like that, something like a manifesto, radiating conviction about women's lives:

> The woman herself may tell it, in what she chooses to call an autobiography; she may tell it in what she chooses to call fiction; a biographer, woman or man, may write the woman's life in what is called a biography; *or the woman may write her own life in advance of living it, unconsciously, and without recognizing or naming the process.*

The fourth way is stylistically different from the other three, and significantly more complex. I've emphasized the fourth way because it's the most original of the categories and contains the kernel of her project in the book. But what exactly did she mean by writing a life unconsciously?

In an autobiographical meditation toward the end of the book, Carolyn explains how she came to create her detective novels, with their glamorous, slender heroine, Kate Fansler:

> All the conscious reasons for writing were good ones; they operated, they were sufficient to explain my actions. Yet the real reasons permitted me, as other women have found ways to permit themselves, to write my own life on a level far below consciousness, making it possible for me to experience what I would not have had the courage to undertake in full awareness.

If Carolyn recognized, in retrospect, that while there were "real reasons" lurking beneath the surface of her conscious mind that mattered as part of a personal accountability, this was not what she was after: "So women like Carolyn Heilbrun in 1963, and writers of an earlier time, seeking some place outside Freud's family romance, wrote out, under other names or in hidden stories, their revolutionary hopes." Carolyn, who typically pooh-poohed psychoanalysis in theory and in practice and referred to dreams as the "detritus of the mind," here willingly assigns a starring role played by unconscious desires at work in women's hopes and stories as they forged a path outside the traps of the conventional family and the scripts laid down for women.

These other women, with other names, like her were enacting what Carolyn called a "quest plot," a way of being in the world not bound to the conventions of feminine destinies (pace Freud). What then was Carolyn herself after? "I sought, I guess, psychic space. But I also sought another identity, another role. . . . I created a fantasy," she wrote. "Creating Kate Fansler and her quests, I was recreating myself."

▨ ▨ ▨

The fourth way still inspires women readers.

The cover image of Kate Bolick's recent memoir, *Spinster: Making a Life of One's Own*, the title of which echoes Woolf's famous essay, features a young woman who looks a lot like Kate Fansler. While I doubt that the designers consciously (though why not?) evoked that fictional character's beauty and elegance, perhaps something of Bolick's interest in *Writing a Woman's Life* emerged as she was looking for language to explain her spinsterhood ideal and its existence in the lives of several women writers. While working at a newspaper in 2003, Bolick explains, she came across Carolyn's obituary, and the following weekend bought a copy of the 1988 book cited there.

"By the time I'd finished reading," she writes, "I'd underlined nearly the entire thing, beginning with the first sentence" and its four ways. Bolick is Carolyn's ideal reader: *"Is this what I've been doing, I tentatively, hopefully wondered, writing my own life, unwittingly, in particular, in advance of living it?"* Bolick feels gratified, recognized, in her reading of the unmarried women who showed her "how to think beyond the marriage plot. The conversations I had with them," she writes, "created the pages that were my life."

The pages that were my life. A pellucid solution to the feedback loop at the heart of the metaphor: living before putting the life on paper.

(This strategy—conscious or not—was characteristic of Carolyn's life in general. In a summer letter from 1981, she gleefully describes the decision to divide her country house in two, resulting in an independent, separate space for her grown children: "Dividing the house was one of those inspirations that, had I created it as a text, would have insured my immortality. As it is, it merely insures my serenity.")

Had I created it as a text.

⊞ ⊞ ⊞

Toward the end of her book, Kate Bolick returns to *Writing a Woman's Life*, pulling out an expression that embodied her "spinster wish," her longing for "avenues of meaning and identity" other than marriage. Carolyn borrowed *ambiguous women* from Stanley Cavell, a reworking of her earlier use of *androgyny*. Bolick embraces the concept for herself: the "wonderful term for those who choose not to center their life around a man—I became one." The phrase that so captivates Kate Bolick as a self-portrait also captures the fascination she experienced writing about the five women whose stories she tells in the book, and how it illuminates her work: "Such is the odd fate, even now, of the feminist project: Progress is so fitful, and went unrecorded for so long, that an idea doesn't have to be new to be eye-opening."

I wished, on reading *Spinster*, mournfully, but also a little angrily, that Carolyn had stayed alive until 2015, living her own ambiguous life on her own terms, long enough to see the afterlife of her idea celebrated and re-embodied by a like-minded young woman who believed in Carolyn's vision of the world and what feminism could bring about.

⊡ ⊡ ⊡

Secrecy was not only a way of keeping the new identity from her colleagues at Columbia; it was also part of the deeper attraction of the Amanda Cross pseudonym: "Secrecy is power." "Secrecy is power" may well be the maxim that guided Carolyn in many more ways than shielding herself from the scorn of colleagues in the years before her own tenure; it was also how she lived her life with friends.

The archives of *Ms.* magazine are held at Smith College. Carolyn's papers are there, too. A few years ago, at the fortieth anniversary celebration of the magazine, I learned, in chatting with the archivists of the collection, that Carolyn had deposited diaries there, the diaries she said she never kept, sealed by the family for thirty-five years. Like the "hidden stories" she deciphered in the lives of other women, she kept these to herself.

The hardest friendship lesson to learn: There will always be something about your friend that remains unknowable, including her deepest feelings about you. Paradoxically, though, friendship is also protected by secrets.

I won't be alive to visit the archives when they are unsealed, but I'm not sure I regret this.

AFFIDAMENTO

Carolyn wrote a new book almost every year, it sometimes seemed. The inscriptions in the copies she gave me tell a kind of friendship story:

Reinventing Womanhood
In Cambridge and New York—in friendship and admiration, Carolyn (Aug. 31, 1980)
Death in a Tenured Position
—For Nancy—Hoping you can find an hour's diversion in anything with "tenure" in the title—Love, Carolyn (March 11, 1981)
Sweet Death, Kind Death
With love and admiration from her friend and co-editor etc. Carolyn
Writing a Woman's Life
—For Nancy—who has greatly helped this woman to write her life—with love and admiration. Carolyn (8 IX 88)
A Trap for Fools
For Nancy, if she can find an idle hour, with love, Carolyn (13 IV 89)
The Players Come Again
For Nancy—should time be hanging heavy on her hands—with much love and admiration, Carolyn (4 X 90)
Hamlet's Mother and Other Women
For Nancy, With love, Carolyn (9 VII 90, at Akaihana)
An Imperfect Spy
For Nancy—To read as mild diversion in a spare moment, if you can find one. Love, C. (1 5 95)
The Education of a Woman: The Life of Gloria Steinem

For Nancy, whose weekly conversations have offered sustenance,
vicarious adventures, and much else. Love, Carolyn (29 VII 95)

The Puzzled Heart

For Nancy, who reads what I write, even if it has a big dog within.
Love, Carolyn

(2 3 98)

The Last Gift of Time

I can't imagine what you'll make of this, but I'm hoping you'll like it.
With Love, Carolyn (17 III 97)

Honest Doubt

For Nancy—another oddity from her odd friend, the author—with
love and thankfulness for her friendship. Amanda (11/22/00)

*When Men Were the Only Models We Had: My Teachers Barzun, Fadi-
man, Trilling*

Marking twenty years of conversation, raw fish, and my gratitude
for your friendship, Carolyn (9.19.01)

The Edge of Doom

For Nancy with love.
"Ah! My good friend, what cheer?" (11.11.02)

Until I assembled the books (and a few had gone missing), I had
not remembered the theme of gratitude. Why did Carolyn express
thankfulness for my friendship in the inscriptions? Shouldn't
it have been, wasn't it, the other way around? (At least I got to
write the foreword to *Hamlet's Mother*.) Italian feminists coined
the term *affidamento* (literally *entrustment*) to mean the relationship between a younger woman and an older woman without the
conventional barriers of hierarchy that structure mentorship.
Sometimes the difference of status erodes over time, but its roots
are difficult to extricate.

I can't help worrying about this difficulty with the young friends in my life, especially Victoria, with whom I now co-edit the Gender and Culture series. She is twenty-seven years younger than I am, almost twice the number of years that separated Carolyn and me. We are very close, but I never seek to erase the realities of the age difference as Carolyn liked to do, nor does Victoria. Carolyn, though, plays a significant role in our friendship. Notably, we have continued the tradition of weekly dinners. I also sometimes channel Carolyn's cranky moods; fortunately, Victoria, who is nothing like me (past or present), doesn't seem to mind.

In the case of Victoria and of the still much younger friends who were also my students, I can't ignore our generational differences, even as I know that they don't always matter; and I often recognize in myself the sense of gratitude for their conversation that Carolyn said she felt with me. But there's more to be explored here, which is implicit, I think, in *affidamento*: Beyond gratitude, or maybe within gratitude, is the joy of renewal, the surprise of the new that only comes from the young. This is the other, much less acknowledged boon to the mentor, less acknowledged because less chartable than whatever advantages mentees derive from the relationship in their career, but no less real.

GIFTS

Objects lead memory.

The only birthday gift from Carolyn no longer in my possession is a bright yellow Sony Discman that, in the early 1990s, I would listen to while jogging around the reservoir in Central Park. The condition for receiving a present from Carolyn was simple: It should be something I would like to have but could not afford: hence the Discman.

That model of gift giving had the advantage, she explained, both of not wasting the time it would take to shop for the right present and of guaranteeing pleasure. Why give the wrong gift, or a gift that would disappoint, if you could determine ahead of time what would be desired?

Above all, Carolyn tried to avoid messy situations if there were a practical solution at hand. If something was amiss at home with one of her children, she would take that child for a walk in Central Park, she said, discussing the issue—resolving it—and relegating it to the past tense. Done. No dark, murky emotions left poisoning the atmosphere, as they did when I was growing up.

When I got married, and Carolyn wanted to give us a wedding present, she took me to Fortunoff, and together we chose a sterling silver serving fork and spoon. They were not actually a pair—neither of us wanted that—but in their sleek, subtle design lines, they were perfectly matched, as if in dialogue with each other. I loved that the silver bore slight traces of many unknown meals, but still looked elegant enough to trot out for company.

That was our only joint shopping excursion for me.

For my sixtieth birthday, Carolyn asked what I longed to own. I chose two large-format black-and-white photographs of Vietnamese landscapes by An-My Lê, whose haunting work I had discovered in the late nineties.

I cherish equally a humbler gift that I touch every day: a multi-colored ceramic salad bowl that combines broad, wavy stripes of red, yellow, purple, and green on the outside and polka dots in the same colors sprinkled over the bright yellow inside. It belonged to an Italian pottery series from Avventura, an upscale gift shop on Amsterdam Avenue with imported glassware and tableware in our old neighborhood; it's gone now, too. Naomi had already given me a pitcher from the series, and I had told Carolyn how much I liked it. The gifts are now related, if not the friends, except in memory.

I was not allowed to combine dots and stripes when I was a child, so the pattern always feels like an aesthetic vindication, however belated. Carolyn found the enjoyment of domestic daily life overrated. I don't love kitchen routines either, but the bowl's aura helps distract me from boredom, though not melancholy: I think of Carolyn whenever I serve salad, which is almost every night.

There was another gift, one that Carolyn engineered, on the occasion of my leaving Barnard for CUNY in 1988. At the time, she was the director of the newly created Institute for Research on Women and Gender (IRWAG, as the unfortunate acronym evolved). The Institute graciously hosted a farewell party for my departure and presented me with two precious objects: an eighteenth-century leather-bound edition of *La Princesse de Clèves*, the seventeenth-century French novel by Madame de La Fayette, a writer Carolyn knew I adored—and a silver tray with ornately carved edges, designed for holding pens. Gifts for a woman who wanted to think of herself as a woman writer. Gifts for the desk.

Perhaps that is finally what all Carolyn's gifts to me did: They validated my ambition and desires beyond the limits I had set for myself.

In "Saying Good-by to Hannah," her eulogy for Hannah Arendt, Mary McCarthy tells a story about inviting her good friend to stay with her—in a separate apartment—in Maine. In honor of her visit, Mary scouted out a tube of anchovy paste in the local grocery store because she knew Hannah liked to have it with her breakfast. Arendt, however, was vexed by the attention. "What is this?" she asked in an irritated voice, as if she had no idea what the tube contained. "Oh," Hannah replied, when given the answer. She did not like, McCarthy concluded, the feeling of being known in her private tastes, even by her beloved friend of twenty-five years. That anecdote feels perversely true, and not just about Hannah Arendt. It can be dangerous to guess what someone else, even an intimate friend, might want.

Carolyn did not make gift giving easy, as there appeared to be nothing she wanted or needed. A Duncan Grant and a Vanessa Bell hung on the walls of her living room. I felt paralyzed by envy and embarrassed by the disparity of scale. What had I to offer? Still, one had to figure out something. It could not be clothing, as I learned the hard way the time I bought her a khaki flak jacket. She ordered what she needed from catalogues and would not reveal her size; plus, everything made her feel hot. In her biography, Susan Kress reports that Carolyn "liked gifts but had not received many as a child," a subject not pursued between the two of them. Door closed, perhaps not the case. She never admitted to needing or wanting anything she couldn't acquire for herself.

I remember now, almost twenty birthdays since her death, a few objects I chose that were useless but attractive and could sit on her desk: a paperweight in Jerusalem stone, tiny figurines from Vietnam—that was late in the game. Desks were a safe space, at least for small objects.

There was also an early twentieth-century French decorative plate with a friendly-looking dog painted on its surface that I brought back from one of my trips to Paris. In "The Small House," the chapter in *The Last Gift of Time* that describes the house Carolyn bought in late life, she declares her intention to "put no pictures on the walls; I wanted it like this: stark, unadorned, comfortable." I was touched to learn from Susan Heath, an intimate friend of Carolyn's and to whom Carolyn left her country house (her last gift), that Carolyn had made an exception for the plate.

Carolyn could, though, accept gifts of time and attention, shopping for new glasses frames, for example, or requesting something she specifically wanted, like thick-cut marmalade from London whenever I traveled there. But there's no getting around it: If I am unable to recall more than these tiny gifts, it is because being Carolyn's friend, for me, meant failing on the literal level of exchange. Her boundaries were sealed to me, as they were to all of us. I was, I remain, remiss.

JIM

The husband of an intimate friend often is not also a friend, at least not necessarily. I doubt that I saw Jim Heilbrun more than a dozen times—that seems a lot—over the years that Carolyn and I met for dinner, even when I came to her apartment for a drink or a meeting. He sometimes poked his head into the living room to check on some domestic detail, but I don't think we ever had a conversation on our own. I can hear his voice, though, which was a bit flat and nasal and inherently calm.

That doesn't mean that I didn't have a sense of Jim, although it was largely based on Carolyn's characterization, the occasional anecdote, and what she wrote about him. I can report, however, that he was quite good looking, slender with dark hair and deep blue eyes. It was not hard to imagine him as the dashing young Navy man she had married when she was just nineteen, while still a student at Wellesley—so that they could have sex, she liked to explain, relentless in venting in retrospect against the rules of 1950s American culture. For Carolyn, their relationship could only be understood not just as a marriage, but as a long marriage, a category she saw as a kind of sane accomplishment in a mad world, as in the film comedies of remarriage from the thirties and forties that she loved. Jim, a distinguished economist, provided balance, Carolyn energy, as she described their couple's emotional equation.

Jim often figured in the conversation between us as a kind of absent, though benign presence. Jim and I, it seems, shared certain habits that made him more like me than like her: feeling cold when others feel hot, being an early riser, and weirdly—why do I remember this?—keeping bread in the refrigerator, something Carolyn

found ridiculous. I always felt a silent bond with Jim over those
minor oddities. Of course you should keep bread in the refrigerator.

⊞ ⊞ ⊞

In the fall of 1992, immediately following Carolyn's fraught departure from Columbia, three of Carolyn's friends—Rachel Brownstein,
Mary Ann Caws, Jane Marcus, and I—all of whom taught at CUNY,
organized a celebration in her honor, when it became clear that
Columbia had no plans to acknowledge her long career there. The
event was sunny and buoyant throughout the day, with hilarious
anecdotes from former students. At the end, as Cole Porter's
"You're the Top" played in the background, Carolyn and her family
came to the stage. As she mounted the steps to the platform, Jim
followed behind like Prince Philip shadowing the Queen and gave
his wife a love tap on the bottom.

To the extent that Jim and their marriage always felt kind of
disembodied (if also a crucial part of Carolyn's identity), the pat
on the bum was a startling and adorable gesture. It was a reminder
of how little we know of the tiny exchanges that take place in a
marriage and how comforting it can be to glimpse them. The tap
showed that Jim was not in awe of Carolyn and that affection was
still currency between them.

THE LAST YEARS OF OUR DINNERS

We were still eating at Akaihana in 2002 when Carolyn published her last mystery, *The Edge of Doom*. She inscribed the novel with a quotation from Shakespeare's bitter play *Timon of Athens*: "Ah, my good friend, what cheer?" I guessed the line had to come from Shakespeare, since the entire book was built around quotations from his plays and sonnets, but it took some research by my friend Rich McCoy, a Shakespeare scholar, to situate the quotation for me: a barb from an embattled ruler to the fair-weather friends he plans to punish for lack of loyalty. I doubt I made anything of it at the time, but this was, I now learned, the opposite of a friendly salutation.

What was happening to our friendship?

⊞ ⊞ ⊞

In 2002, the Columbia English department, which Carolyn had left a decade earlier, was still in such turmoil that in March of that year, the *Times* ran a story about the internal conflicts roiling the department. It reported that she had left "in a huff," prompting an indignant letter to the editor. In " 'Huff,' Deconstructed," Carolyn wrote, with characteristic arch, that the article "seemed to imply that only women can leave in a huff. In a huff I may have been, but there were men in the department, some who left and some who stayed, who gave 'huff' a whole new meaning beyond my talents."

"In a huff I may have been." In reality, the huff was more like rage, still hot in the years before her suicide; it comes out in her 2000 mystery, *Honest Doubt*, in which an entire English department does in an irritating colleague, and in her 2001 memoir, *When Men*

Were the Only Models We Had, in which she revisits her education and career at Columbia in the era of Lionel Trilling.

In 2002, I published *But Enough About Me*, a collection of autobiographical essays I had written in the 1990s that began as a book about the 1950s. (One might note—I do—the disparity between Carolyn's book production schedule and my own.) In some ways, *But Enough* remained a book about the fifties: I was interested in figuring out how girls like me became seventies feminists, and how, twenty years or so later, we remained so. Upon reading the manuscript, Carolyn commented, blandly, over dinner, that an essay tracing my life as a feminist academic had not mentioned her role in my career. There was a blank where that story might have been told, and with it a telling of the ways in which, like Athena guiding Odysseus, she had kept me from hitting the rocks, upending the voyage.

I went back and added a parenthesis about her mentorship in a paragraph.

I don't remember what she said when I showed her the paragraph, but I could tell that she was still disappointed. The French have an expression, "du bout des lèvres," meaning something like "lip service." I was paying my dues, no more. I still can't fully say why, why I had left her out, why that was not the story I wanted to tell.

My ingratitude. Maybe I was the one who didn't want to think of her as a mentor.

One dinner in July, before we parted for the summer, soon after the book was out, I asked Carolyn what she thought of it. "What do you want me to say?" she asked. "That it's the greatest thing since bottled beer? It's a collection of essays." (Bottled beer, alternately sliced bread, two of Carolyn's cherished dismissals, after my favorite, modified rapture.) We continued in wounded silence, face to face. She was angry. That I had not presented her with a signed copy of the book, as she always did with hers. That, at my suggestion, we now met only every other week. Her hair stood on end in wisps, escaping from her bun in the July humidity. "You're shouting," I said. "You're shouting in your own way," she retorted. The waiters hovered nervously. The weird solo eater looked up from his plate to stare at us, for the first time in our common eating history. We paid the check and left the restaurant, not talking.

We resumed our weekly dinners in the fall, keeping them up until I left New York the following year for my sabbatical. Over the summer, I finished the draft of the Paris memoir I had started and stopped writing too many times and dropped off a copy with the doorman at her apartment building. Carolyn was enthusiastic. "You have done it at last," she wrote in an email. "It's an extraordinary record of that time and that place." She did not live long enough after that vote of confidence to learn that the memoir would not find a publisher for another ten years, but I don't think she would have given up on me.

Did her approval of the memoir make her feel that she had stood by me long enough? That I no longer needed her? I oscillate wildly between thinking I didn't matter to the timing of the suicide and I mattered too much. In either case, it's all much too much about me.

I was not, of course, the only woman with whom Carolyn had dinner during the week on a regular basis—there were other women friends, male friends of long date, and the occasional wild card, the visitor from out of town, or a professional acquaintance.

I'm not sure Carolyn dined out every weekday night, though I suspect that she would have been happy to. And there were also the friends with whom she walked. Walking while talking (alternately walking the dog) was her preferred daytime activity when she wasn't home reading and writing alone, teaching and seeing students at Columbia, prior to her retirement, or, when it was the season, watching baseball.

I have contradictory feelings about the schedule that I can't quite untangle: I felt, Carolyn always made me feel, that our dinners were very important to her; at the same time, I knew other friends on the calendar also mattered. Naturally, you'll say, that's the nature of friendship. It's not exclusive, it's not marriage. Although my place in Carolyn's life was also marked by the generosity with which she quoted my academic work, and by the fond inscriptions to her many books, I never assumed that I had a special place in the repertory. Yet others seemed to feel we were a pair of sorts, and the many condolence notes I received after her suicide assumed that her death would be my particular loss: condolences for an intimate friend's death, a new genre. In the aftermath, that somehow seemed right. It does now.

For most of her life, routines served Carolyn well. She had created an order suited to her temperament and organized her space to reflect that. She often boasted about having a clean desk and clearing her inbox, a trait she said came from her father. If you have a job to do, give it to a busy person was his motto, and then hers. Only in the final years, when the desk was often empty of tasks, did that motto feel cruel.

I keep my desk a mess to guard against the vision of emptiness, looking busy.

ALONE IN THE HOLE

In his *Roland Barthes by Roland Barthes*, the critic recalls an unhappy scene from childhood. He was playing with other children from his neighborhood in a hole dug out of the ground on an empty building site until "all the children climbed out, except me—I couldn't make it." The children, looking down at the boy, tease him mercilessly, until finally his mother arrives to rescue him from his solitary confinement. The memory of solitude is a painful instance of the feeling Barthes names exclusion: "To be excluded is not to be outside, it is to be *alone in the hole*." I'm always riven by this entry because it's a tiny island of vulnerability in a sea of complicated, sometimes convoluted, meditations on what it means for the iconic high-theory French intellectual to compose an autobiography without getting too personal.

No one is coming to save me, I think in a flash of identification, least of all my mother. I'm going to have to scramble out by myself.

Carolyn called the sense of misery that overcame her whenever she returned to her alma mater, always reluctantly, when summoned for some event on behalf of women, "doing a Wellesley." "When that happens, I want to go into the garden and eat worms," she'd say. In the face of this unhappiness, Jim would spring into action and "man the pumps," an expression from his days in the Navy.

The solitude of the hole attracts and frightens writers. Carolyn described its power in the period leading up to her suicide, in what turned out to be the last essay she published in her lifetime, a commissioned piece in the *Women's Review of Books* on the subject of aging. In "Taking a U-Turn: The Aging Woman as Explorer of New

Territory," she cites a passage from Marguerite Duras, quoted in turn by Margaret Atwood, that conjures the panic of the hole as a quintessential writer's dilemma: "Finding yourself in a hole, at the bottom of a hole, in almost total solitude, and discovering that only writing can save you. To be without the slightest subject for a book." Duras, Carolyn comments dryly in the essay, "perfectly describes the situation" of the aging woman writer. "I fear living with the certainty," she wrote, "that there is no further work demanding to be done."

Atwood uses the Duras quotation as an epigraph to her book of essays *Negotiating with the Dead: A Writer on Writing*, in which she cites the French writer more fully. After invoking the despair of being "without the slightest subject for a book," Duras strikes another note, a measure of repair and hope: To be without a subject for a book "is to find yourself, once again, before a book." Carolyn cut off the return to writing, using the oddly inelegant "U-turn" metaphor, turning her back on her former self.

Alone in the hole.

In *Writing*, the book from which Atwood quotes, Duras says significantly more, about both the terror of there not being another book and the anguish of having to begin again: "A vast emptiness. A possible book. Before nothing." She describes the solitude of this moment in time in which one book has been written and published and the next has yet to come: "To be alone with the as yet unwritten book . . . also means being alone with the writing that is still lying fallow." Carolyn was no stranger to that idea. You have to wait until the well fills up again, she used to say, her wisdom to me. But a few months before her suicide, she seemed to have settled into life in the hole.

Why now the conviction that this mysterious exit from the road of the long wait was permanently closed? "Taking a U-Turn" signaled the end of what she was to call the journey.

The essay describes a project of reading about men of science, rather than women of letters, paradigms of scientific knowledge rather than those of the feminism that had animated her for so long. Would this fascination become a book, or would it remain a velleity? "I must write," she concludes, "but only for myself," a conclusion that sounds hollow, even untrue. "Is that, I ask myself, because, were I to attempt to publish, I would have to fear rejection?" Although Carolyn appears to shrug off that eventuality—"Yes, there is that, but not as much of that as there might be"—she has, at the same time, conjured the specter of rejection's power to inflict pain.

Rejection, criticism, there had been. There were harsh reviews in the mid-eighties of her Gloria Steinem biography (a project Carolyn in retrospect considered a mistake), and early on, a stingingly negative evaluation of her 1979 *Reinventing Womanhood* in the *New York Times*. The bad *Times* review did not kill the book or the author, but the phone, Carolyn said, didn't ring for a month. She continued to be admired, lionized, invited, solicited, quoted, and envied, though her importance, she had come to believe, belonged to a past tense, even a past self.

I recognized the tone of flat-out discouragement that I had heard over the years from Carolyn at dinner, but I was shocked to read it in published form, almost as a manifesto. There had always been the renewal that came from another book, the essays and stories, the Amanda Cross mysteries. I had never heard the anxiety about writing expressed with so much violence, especially the conviction of placing herself beyond rescue.

In the cruelest of ironies, the disappointment Carolyn thought she'd risk in writing about science was to come, not long after she published her essay about women and aging in the *Women's Review of Books*, from an unexpected quarter.

Most of Carolyn's autobiographical writing took the form of short personal essays, sometimes collected in a book, sometimes punctuating arguments in books with other subjects, notably a chapter in *Reinventing Womanhood*, "Woman as Outsider," in which she described the chilly climate for women at Columbia before affirmative action. But when invited to write for a new series from the University of Pennsylvania Press called "Personal Takes," Carolyn composed a memoir with a clear autobiographical aim: *When Men Were the Only Models We Had: My Teachers Barzun, Fadiman, Trilling*, published in 2002, the year before her death. The book re-creates her years at Columbia in the 1950s as a graduate student and then a young faculty member in the English department. The memoir draws portraits of the three men whose teaching and writing shaped her intellectual world even as they seemed to exclude her from it.

The recollection, fifty years later, is bittersweet: "Looking back upon them is to be transported to another world. Reading about them since those first years has once again made me understand that men cannot, ultimately, offer women complete patterns for their lives." And yet, as she shows in the memoir, these men, whatever their limitations, offered a "pattern of the intellectual life." Still, Columbia continued to be the scene of a persistent sense of exclusion, like the traumatic reopening of a wound, despite the fact that she became a named professor, overlapping briefly in her career in the English department with Lionel Trilling and Jacques Barzun.

Carolyn must have been disappointed in the reviews of the memoir because she asked me to review it. This was wholly out of character for Carolyn, and out of our habits as friends, one of the very few times she asked me for help. I was eager to repay my debt and reviewed the memoir in *Signs*, along with *Fireweed*, a recent autobiography by the historian Gerda Lerner, another feminist pioneer, a few years younger than Carolyn. When the review appeared the following year, it was framed by a brief obituary.

She had inscribed the copy to me: "Marking twenty years of conversation, raw fish, and my gratitude for your friendship," September 19, 2001.

The question of gratitude, as Joan Didion might say.

▣ ▣ ▣

At the end of August 2003, I left for a sabbatical year in London. Carolyn and I met at Café Louis, a local hangout at Amsterdam and 80th Street, rather than our usual sushi restaurant, for a farewell dinner. Or maybe it wasn't for dinner, but just a drink, contrary to our rituals. I looked for Carolyn, who was always on time, even early, and found her sitting almost huddled in a corner near the window facing 80th Street. She was pale against her black tunic, drained by the hot, sticky weather that she hated, looking reproachful, or at least impatient, because I was, despite good intentions, late. It was noisy because of the bar scene, and we strained to hear each other. We were saying good-bye, but not for long, right? I was serving on the Executive Council of the MLA and had promised to fly back for some meetings. I had brought my date book with me, looking ahead to my return to New York in October. Carolyn seemed distracted. Of course we'd see each other, but there was time to fix a date; it almost seemed as if finding a date was an imposition. Since dates with Carolyn were always specific, even rigidly set, I was surprised by her reluctance to decide. She apologized and asked me to forgive an "old party." When she uttered that expression, the kind of slightly antiquated British phrasing she was attracted to, she seemed suddenly frail. I offered to walk her home, but she waved me off; it was too hot, I should go home and finish packing, she'd be fine.

In September, as I began planning my visit to New York, I began again trying to fix a date with her by email. She put me off:

9/23/2003, 3:53:22 p.m. GMT Daylight Time

Dear Nancy

It looks as though I won't be able to have a visit with you on this trip. Why don't we make a phone date, as you are doing with Victoria, and we can have a good talk then?

In the aftermath of the suicide, when I printed Carolyn's emails, it had not occurred to me to preserve mine. I'm not even sure now why I printed hers, except to think that I would be struggling to understand for a long time to come what moved her to act when she did. At the time, though, while I don't remember exactly how I answered that message, I imagine that I objected to the suggestion that we speak by phone transatlantically. (Victoria—a mutual friend and Carolyn's former student as well as mine—lived in Texas.) If I was in New York, I wanted to see Carolyn in person.

I must have protested, because she continued to mount a defense against our meeting:

9/23/2003 7:29 GMT Daylight Time

I'm afraid I can't plan anything now. I don't feel satisfied
with brief visits. Please don't be impatient with me.
Unlike your great children, I'm an old party and as you
have always said, cranky.

Love, Carolyn

Reading these messages now, I'm overwhelmed with a sense of my failure to understand what I was reading. Did the allusion to brief meetings refer to our last, hurried drinks at Café Louis? The self-designated "old party" was exactly the phrase she had used about herself that evening. I must have bristled, I still do, at Carolyn's calling my younger friends, often former graduate students like Victoria, my "great children." I could not fathom why, suddenly, she did not want to see me. And so we wrangled on, each consolidating her position.

Why did I have to press so hard for a date one month away?

◼ ◼ ◼

When Men Were the Only Models We Had was published in hardcover only; the publishers did not foresee a paperback edition. I loved the book and hoped we might bring out a paperback version in our series at Columbia:

9/28/2003 7:00 GMT Daylight Time

The Press has turned down my book for paperback.
Perhaps at a certain point in life . . . it doesn't matter
whether you die or not.

I was not reading the signs emanating from New York:

9/28/2003 7:00 GMT Daylight Time

Dear N.

Thanks for the sympathy. I'm really sad. It seems there's
a faculty committee policy against doing paperbacks
of other publishers' books and the Press said the book
wouldn't sell for more than 500 in paperback. I will
forbear commenting on this nonsense.

I was reading the messages on the top floor of the three-story,
book-filled flat I had rented, looking out at the rooftops of London against a gray horizon. It did it not occur to me to pick up
the phone and commiserate, and I don't now believe a call would
have changed anything. It was as though, as Mary Ann Caws, one
of Carolyn's oldest walking friends, said to me recently, the pub-
lishing disappointment, like an accident waiting to happen, helped
move her, after years of deferral, to putting the long-planned act,
declared and justified, elegantly in print, on the calendar.

Some decisions trump, and necessarily betray, any intimacy or
love because they require the ultimate withdrawal of self. Perhaps
that removal is the definition of suicide, what in German is called

self-murder; the friendship that requires two selves is just another casualty.

⊞ ⊞ ⊞

10/1/2003 5:41:48 GMT Daylight Time

A wry note. I may see you after all on the weekend you are here. I have been invited as an ex-President, to join the Executive Council for dinner on Friday, Oct. 24. God or whoever moves in mysterious ways. Perhaps we can get in a moment beforehand. Or not, as I know you will be very busy.

Love, C.

We never saw each other again.

SUICIDE

See you tomorrow, you said. You lied.

—Maxine Kumin, "Splitting Wood at Six Above"

Carolyn killed herself on a Thursday in October, though it might have been a Wednesday; the autopsy was not definitive about the date. Thursday, however, was dinner with Susan Heath—the friends followed a weekly rotation—and Susan was the one chosen by Carolyn to find her body when she arrived for their date. The doorman let her into the apartment, Susan told me, when no one answered the doorbell. Carolyn was lying, fully dressed, on her bed, she said, a plastic bag pulled over her head. Carolyn had planned her death for too long to risk failure.

Susan called me in London. We spoke briefly, with a twinned sense of shock and resignation. Of course she went through with it; why did we ever think Carolyn would not act on her decision as announced? But still. I did not ask Susan what Carolyn's face looked like seen through the bag. I imagined her expression, if legible, as determined but peaceful. I hoped she felt bliss at the imminent release, not merely the bitter satisfaction of keeping her word, of being right.

All these years later, bitterness, it seems, is mine. Bitterness, but sadness, too, and also fear that I have grown close to her despair, gripped by a writer's panic, the terror of having written a last book, this one. Or perhaps she was tired of occupying the mentor position, as another mutual friend suggested, locked as she was into a stance of invulnerability, unable to reveal the wound, the need for reassurance, after so many years of wearing the mentor mask.

"The journey is over," she wrote. "Love to all, Carolyn." (All or none, we all thought we deserved a note of our own.)

How can you tell when the journey is over? This was a question Carolyn had been asking herself for many years, publicly, in print. In the preface to *The Last Gift of Time*, her elegiac book about aging published in 1997, she expressed her intention to commit suicide, a "determination" that she had settled on "long ago," as a definitive gesture of autonomy. But when would it be time? Seventy, she had thought at first. Then when seventy passed, she decided that she would wait until the moment seemed right: "Each day one can say to oneself: I can always die; do I choose death or life?" In the end, it was seventy-seven, the same age as her mother at her death.

Follow the mentor. As I pass the age Carolyn had decided was a good enough age to die, I can't help wondering whether it's not my time, too.

CAROLYN AND VIRGINIA

Carolyn's last essay was published posthumously. It was an invited piece for an issue of the journal *PMLA* on the theme of rereading that appeared in 2004 as a guest column and that she had described to me as "frivolous sounding and most unscholarly," adding, "I don't think that they can use it."

"Rereading is much recommended to those for whom time is, as Virginia Woolf once put it, flapping around one," Carolyn wrote in the opening moves of the essay that reflects upon Henry James's novel *The Ambassadors* and its portrait of the aging character Strether. The phrase of "time flapping" recurs throughout her work in various guises. In *Writing a Woman's Life*, she had invoked it to suggest that we academics shouldn't allow ourselves to become static in our lives once we achieve a measure of security, but rather strike out and try something bold and courageous.

Woolf, though, first created the "flapping" metaphor to describe attacks of melancholy and their relation to writing and creativity, not aging, in a 1920 diary entry when she was thirty-eight, "Monday, October 25 (first day of winter time)":

> Why is life so tragic; so like a little strip of pavement over an abyss. I look down; I feel giddy; I wonder how I am ever to walk to the end. . . . Its a feeling of impotence: of cutting no ice . . . Melancholy diminishes as I write. . . . I think too much of whys and wherefores: too much of myself. I dont like time to flap round me.

Five years later, in *Mrs. Dalloway*, the image works a bit differently:

> As a cloud crosses the sun, silence falls on London; and falls on the mind. Effort ceases. Time flaps on the mast. There we stop; there we stand. Rigid, the skeleton of habit alone upholds the human frame.

A third use of the phrase appears on Saturday, June 15, 1929:

> Pinker has just come home, very fat. And a sense of nothingness rolls about the house. . . . Time flaps on the mast, my own phrase I think. . . . Time flaps on the mast. And then I see through everything. Perhaps the image ought to have been one that gives an idea of a stream becoming thin: of seeing to the bottom.

Rather than remaining immobilized by melancholia, Woolf persisted as a writer, and in the diary recalls a conversation with Lytton Strachey, noting how, in the course of the conversation, she came to no longer envy him, thinking that she had outdone him with *Orlando*, and now it was his turn to experience envy. That brings the phrase back again in the same entry:

> Now time must not flap on the mast any more. Now I must somehow brew another decoction of illusion. Well, if the human interest flags— if its that that worries me, I must not sit thinking about it here.

The following entry, dated Sunday, June 16, picks up the trail of the metaphor, explaining that just as she had written those words, Leonard interrupted her. She notes, "The sail filled out again and the ship went on." But then a week later, the melancholia returns:

> And so I pitched into my great lake of melancholy. Lord how deep it is! What a born melancholiac I am! The only way I keep afloat is by working . . . no, I dont know where it comes from. Directly I stop working I feel that I am sinking. Down, down.

But then, sounding like Marguerite Duras emerging from despair to find herself before another book, she states, "And as usual, I feel that if I sink further, I shall reach the truth."

Carolyn recognized Woolf's mood in herself—the panic that sets in when one isn't working—which is why she borrowed the metaphor of flapping time, not once, but twice, when she came to write about retirement. She described her version of that mood in "Sadness," a meditation derived not from Woolf's words but from Shakespeare's. Quoting Antonio's lines from *The Merchant of Venice* about the puzzle of sadness that seems to come unbidden, she meditated on the intensity of the emotion, likening it to melancholy, a temperament, and specifically refusing the term *depression*: melancholy, a mood that comes and goes mysteriously.

For many years, when Carolyn and I talked about depression—notably mine—she would say that, unlike me, she didn't really suffer from it because anything—a sunny day, piece of good news, a friendly phone call—could get her out of that feeling of sinking, being paralyzed, cutting no ice. But then, as Woolf recounted, for Carolyn, too, "the sail filled out again."

In her late-life loneliness, which I think was extreme, Carolyn took not only inspiration from Woolf's courage but also solace from her example as a melancholic and a suicide. In a way, Carolyn's suicide was the act of quotation turned into performance.

Fifteen years after *Writing a Woman's Life*, in which she had deployed the metaphor of time flapping on the mast as a call to action, the specter of time flapping on the mast led instead to the decision to choose suicide. "She chose to end her life before the chance to make that decision for herself could be taken from her," Carolyn argued in "Woolf in Her Fifties." She embraced Woolf's act, the fact that "having totted up the score," the writer "decided that death was the way for her." Carolyn, who liked, in her words, to quit while she was ahead, had come to believe that the sail would not fill out again, and that even if it did, it would not be for a future voyage. The journey was over.

PICTURES FROM AN INSTITUTION

In 2005 three years after her death, and fourteen years after she retired from the university, a conference organized by IRWAG and three colleagues from the Columbia English Department—Lila Abu-Lughod, Marianne Hirsch, and Jean Howard—honored Carolyn and her legacy: "Writing a Feminist's Life: Academics and Their Memoirs." Participants were asked to talk about the role of memoir in our lives as feminists, since the genre had been one Carolyn practiced in a variety of forms. I began by moving back in time to "Decades," a piece composed in response to a question posed by Gayle Greene and Coppélia Kahn, literary critics and editors of the anthology that in 1993 became *Changing Subjects: The Making of Feminist Literary Criticism*. They asked us to describe what led to our becoming feminist scholars and how our feminism shaped our writing and teaching about literature.

The question came in the form of a letter inviting those of us who belonged to a generation that had "come of age" emotionally in the psychic space of the 1950s and 1960s, and professionally in the upheaval of the 1970s, to reflect on that passage. They were looking, the editors explained, for "personal, anecdotal stories" that we were then to "*theorize*" (their italics) "so as to bring out their historical and political dimensions." (We still believed in theory.) They wanted stories that said "I" but in a way that added up to "we." In my story, I described the decision to write a dissertation about the fictional destiny of women in the eighteenth-century novel as something literary, but also covertly autobiographical. I saw myself leaving behind the tendency of my younger self to copy the heroines of novels in which the women were victims (or brides, or both) in order to become a different kind of heroine, leaving the plots of seduction and betrayal behind, writing myself into a new narrative, becoming the heroine of my life.

🞐 🞐 🞐

In the afterword she wrote for *Changing Subjects*, Carolyn sets herself apart from the contributors to the book by generation:

> To me, roughly a decade and a half older than these women, the stories are both strange and achingly familiar. . . . By the 1950s . . . I was already married, having children . . . and organizing my life around them. . . . Those years are largely a blur, but I remember when I was teaching full-time at Brooklyn College, a man asked me what I did with my children while teaching: I told him I locked them in a closet. Or perhaps I only *wanted* to tell him that. Anger seethed, and went on seething until the seventies and early eighties.

I loved the story about locking the children in the closet and often told it whenever the subject of women academics and children emerged in conversation.

In the seventies and eighties, Carolyn explains, her life and the lives of the women writing in this collection coincided with the burgeoning of feminism in the academy. This brought some belated consolation, but she goes on to lambaste Columbia for not understanding that the world was changing, especially when the English department "threatens to turn down for tenure a brilliant feminist woman." This was the catalytic event that brought Carolyn to the decision to retire early.

Writing *before* the department's decision not to tenure Susan Winnett, the young woman in question, Carolyn reviews her life as a feminist in somewhat disturbing terms:

> Columbia has stopped hurting me, but like someone who has escaped a battering marriage—and the analogy is, in many ways, not a far-fetched one for feminist women faculty—I cannot wipe out the terrible years. I cannot change the isolation of all my time at Columbia. But the friendships I have found among women, and what is still referred to as my private life, have made that isolation, if not welcome then benign as a tumor is benign: it's not cancerous, but it doesn't do anyone any good.

Rereading this passage now horrifies me, well more than when Carolyn was alive, when I was inured to her rhetoric about the awfulness of Columbia because I knew it firsthand myself. In retrospect, I can't help thinking that the years of suffering must have wounded Carolyn enough to lead her to choose the metaphor of domestic abuse—something so implausibly remote from her own married life—that makes her sound like a victim of post-traumatic stress disorder. A few months after writing the afterword, Carolyn left Columbia in a very public fashion. In retelling her life here—which she did more than once and in more than one way—the narrative of feminism Carolyn produces is not the triumph of belonging and community, but a chronicle of consolation and change, occasions for joy, and, to a degree, a process of repair.

◫ ◫ ◫

Around the time of the conference at Columbia, I had dinner with Rachel Kranz, a novelist who had been a brilliant student of Carolyn's but decided not to go on for the Ph.D. She had just turned fifty. The two women had been having dinner once a month for several years. We talked about the suicide and what it meant to us, for us, after so many years. Rachel shared her thoughts on the subject with me a few days later:

> We don't have to hold her final action in high regard, no matter how much we regard her work. Nor do we have to denigrate her work because we don't agree with that final action. If she taught us anything, it was that women who could write new lives, couldn't necessarily live them—and vice versa. For me, personally as a writer, that is very liberating. It means I'm allowed to imagine beyond what I'm capable of achieving. If someone else reads what I write and lives beyond what I could live, I've done my work. And so, I think, she's done hers.

Rachel, who loved life, died in 2017 from ovarian cancer.

The conference, I think, would have satisfied Carolyn's sense of poetic justice (an Amanda Cross title from 1970): eight academic women talking about their feminist lives in Philosophy Hall, where she had fought so many battles on behalf of the women at Columbia. I would have liked to remind her that I had spent many hours in this very lounge as a graduate student in the years before I knew her, consuming cookies along with the tea poured from a large copper (if memory serves) urn by faculty wives. I wondered, as I smoked with friends in the late afternoons, whether we would ever succeed in a world in which faculty wives dramatically outnumbered women faculty.

⊞ ⊞ ⊞

When Carolyn left Columbia—she was forced to say "retired" when she wanted to say "resigned"—she almost reveled in a show of pique. Her anger at being betrayed by a male colleague who had promised to support a feminist hire, which would have meant the appointment of a potential ally and friend, became the motor for her departure. She was elated, if also bitter, at leaving the institution that for so many years had been a source of pain. She had to get "out of hating range," as Maxine Hong Kingston wrote in her memoir about her younger self's need to leave home.

I didn't need to read (reread) Carolyn's last two essays to know that she retired too early—too early for her, perhaps for anyone, unless there's something you are burning to do. At seventy-seven, it still feels too early for me, not least in terms of Carolyn's question to herself, one she could not answer: What are you going to do when you can't keep doing what you know how to do? The question terrifies me.

Living with cancer changes one's relation to time, as well as to death. Writing this book is my way of making that time last.

⊞ ⊞ ⊞

In 2014, Susan Gubar, a great long-distance friend of mine, and also a close friend of Carolyn's, asked me if I had read a novel by Brian Morton, *Florence Gordon*. I hadn't, but she persuaded me that the book was really about Carolyn. The novel arrived festooned with blurbs by eminent feminists, and its main character, I thought, was uncannily like Carolyn in late life. Morton had captured her love of literary quotation, impatience with stupidity, suspicions that the young were not like us at all, her tics, quirks, and tastes, her position in the feminist world. There was not another Carolyn.

One passage in the novel, in particular, reminded me eerily of the last time I had seen Carolyn, of how for the first time she had seemed frail and fragile, and not particularly happy to see me—like Florence Gordon, described in the novel as "spiritless, wan, and remote." It felt to the character, a granddaughter who had come for a conversation, "as if Florence was breaking up with *her*." Above all, like Carolyn, Morton's heroine kills herself, although unlike her apparent counterpart, she does so in response to the diagnosis of a terminal illness. After Carolyn died, people wondered: Had she been ill? As far as we know, she had not. We want suicide to have a reason, and illness serves as one—a good reason to die. Why prolong suffering for oneself and others? We are less comfortable with rational suicide, announced, prepared, defended in advance, carried out with clarity and little mess.

Relatively few succeed in enacting the desire to die when faced with a terminal illness. But to die without the diagnosis is rarer still. In all her writing, Carolyn made the argument that, as women, we should be able to control our lives. For her, this meant the end of life as we can—through contraception and abortion—control the beginning. In other words, she saw her decision as an expression of feminist autonomy, a bookend, as it were, to the demand for reproductive rights.

Was she hiding a diagnosis after all? Or simply following her plan to end her life based on her own plot as already written?

Either way, I wanted to be the friend to whom she told everything, with whom she censored nothing. I wasn't. None of us were.

▣ ▣ ▣

I wrote to the novelist and asked him whether he had known Carolyn. He said no. I believed him.

Naomi Schor

Dear Friend, from my life I write to you in your life . . .

—Yiyun Li, *Dear Friend, from My Life I Write to You in Your Life*

2
Naomi

STARTING OUT IN THE SEVENTIES

So I was second in everything. I hoped
that no one would ever realize it.

—Elena Ferrante, *My Brilliant Friend*

Naomi and I almost met in Paris in the late sixties when we
were in our twenties. She was doing research for her dissertation
on the novels of Émile Zola; her boyfriend occasionally worked for
the man I had just married. My husband had created a small, seat-
of-the-pants English language school. One night, the boyfriend and
the husband traveled out of town for a "gig," as they liked to say, borrowing the vocabulary of jazz musicians, pretending they weren't
teachers of English, giving lessons to French upper-management
businessmen who worked in the suburbs for big American oil com-
panies. *Gig* made them feel cool. They were late getting home one
night, probably out drinking at a Vin et Charbons café in some

fringy, working-class neighborhood near the outskirts of Paris, talking about revolution. Both were ardent Marxists, high on Mao.

When she phoned, worried where her boyfriend was, Naomi said we had met at one of the annual restaurant dinners my husband used to host for the teachers. I must have been too caught up in my role as the boss's wife to notice her.

▦ ▦ ▦

It was the beginning of the seventies when we met face to face in New York, at Columbia. We were women between stories. I was no longer living in Paris, no longer the boss's wife—or anybody else's. Naomi had a new boyfriend, but the main connection between us wasn't the men. What counted was her rank as assistant professor in the French department, where I was a graduate student. I was two years older than Naomi, though distinctly below her on the academic ladder. On the other hand, she always said my thesis would surely be publishable (if I managed ever to write one, of course), whereas her Yale dissertation, according to the *éminence grise* of the department, who was also my advisor, belonged in the past tense. For a book, she would have to start over. Naomi thought that his judgment erased any advantage she might have over me in our future careers.

I did not miss the fact that Naomi was my sister's age, almost to the month. I struggled not to envy her, as I had my sister. I sometimes succeeded. We were feminists, after all. We did not believe in penis envy, and we did not believe in feminine rivalry.

Deuce would have been the perfect score if only we had been playing tennis.

Of course, we were not playing tennis, and the game doesn't end at deuce. Its equilibrium is only temporary. Ultimately, someone triumphs. Neither of us wanted to win if it meant the other had to lose. But our friendship was forged in the competitive politics of the university, which is always about winning and losing. From the beginning, within the confines of the French department, there was never room for the two of us; in reality, there was no room for any of the junior women.

Naomi and I were desperately and equally ambitious about our careers as French scholars, though we specialized in the literature of different centuries: mine the eighteenth, hers the nineteenth. Our literary heroines were, of course, French and fated to meet disaster. Hers was Emma Bovary, mine the Marquise de Merteuil. Like them, we were alternately exalted and wounded in our love affairs.

As long as we were both miserable, the balancing act worked. The differences in years and rank mattered less than what we shared: We didn't have what we wanted. The gap between what we lacked and what we wanted—tenure, a relationship (with a man capable of commitment), a child (eventually)—seemed reducible only by a miracle in our favor. We didn't believe in miracles. On the other hand, we believed in each other.

I had never before had a friendship in which I shared the work. It's also true that before Naomi, I had no work to share. From the beginning, we read each other. From the beginning, Naomi was The Friend.

⬚ ⬚ ⬚

Naomi liked to compare us, how we were alike and unalike, including in our appearance. Because we were about the same size and height, when we shopped together we often bought variants of the same piece of clothing—the same sweater with different necklines, the same tunic in different colors—hers always more vivid (aubergine) than mine (beige, a color of insecurity Naomi could not fathom). Our first stop was always Charivari, a boutique on the Upper West Side that carried a limited number of brands, all severely beyond our budget but equally irresistible; it was almost impossible not to find something to buy, including the holy grail of perfectly cut black pants or anything in velvet.

It was not about dressing like twins, exactly; it was a matter of sharing a taste, though we smiled enigmatically when people asked if we were sisters—especially one time, when Naomi cut her long, thick hair, got a very bad perm, and ended up with hair as frizzy as mine, which disconcerted both of us. "There was something intangible and even spooky between us," Gail Caldwell writes of the intensity of her relationship with Caroline Knapp, "that could make strangers mistake us as sisters or lovers." Since Naomi and I each had a sister, our amusement at being taken for sisters was more about seeing the intimacy of our relationship reflected in the eyes of outsiders than wanting to be part of the same biological family. It was enough to share an initial.

I've never thought it a good idea to confuse friends with sisters, and we didn't. At the same time, I can remember feeling that there was something familial (reassuring but oddly exciting because the relationship had been chosen) about wearing the earrings created by my friend's mother, not least, perhaps, because Naomi didn't. She wore her mother's elaborately designed rings instead.

Because we wanted so much from each other, gave and meant so much, I've always known that writing about Naomi would be hard. This friendship gave my life the shape it took after thirty. At the very least, our shared apprenticeship at Columbia in the 1970s had everything to do with the career each of us ultimately had in academia, a path I can't imagine having taken alone. It is also true that while the curriculum vitae, the career narrative, our coming to writing, and our entrance into the professional world, were never the whole of the story, the blood, guts, and nerves of our bond, the place and everything it stood for, formed the background against which our story took shape. What bound us together, though, was something else, something about how we lived and narrated our friendship to each other. Reading Elena Ferrante's astonishing Neapolitan tetralogy helped me understand what that binding agent was and why its power has not abated in memory.

It must seem crazy, I realize, to see mirrored in the saga of two girls from working-class families in postwar Naples the relationship of two middle-class, New York Jewish girls enamored of things French. But for me the heart of the matter justifies the transplant. Crazier still, I think Naomi would agree.

▣ ▣ ▣

In the prologue to *My Brilliant Friend*, the first volume of Ferrante's quartet, we learn that Lila, the narrator's lifelong friend, seems to have disappeared without a trace at the age of sixty-six. Elena, the narrator, known in their milieu as Lenù, is furious: "We'll see who wins this time, I said to myself. I turned on the computer and began to write—all the details of our story, everything that still remained in my memory." And she does so, over the course of four volumes. The intense friendship between the two women unfolds from childhood, through adolescence and adulthood, until this point of dissolution in late middle age, when Elena begins to write the book we read.

I was instantly hooked by the title of the first volume: *My Brilliant Friend*. Of the two, who is the brilliant friend? That question animates the struggle between the two girls: schoolmates, adolescents, then women and mothers. On the day of her wedding, Lila, having refused at sixteen to continue her education, choosing instead to marry, bestows the accolade on Lenù: "You're my brilliant friend, you have to be the best of all, boys and girls." But here's the rub: Brilliant student or not, in her own eyes Lenù loses in comparison to Lila as a writer and as a woman. The two women need each other's approval, sometimes desperately; they also need to see each other as successful in order to feel they exist: "I *want* you to do better," Lila sobs, after reading Lenù's most recent book, which has disappointed her, "because who am I if you aren't great, who am I?" And Elena remembers Lila as having "reinforced her role" as the "mirror" of her "inabilities."

The pair's emotional seesaw of evaluating, judging, and comparing, was the lifeline between Naomi and me for more than twenty years.

Be my mirror, for better or for worse. Who finally is the brilliant friend?

How do we know who we are, if not in relation? Sometimes our mothers tell us, but this is not always the most reliable perception. "You're so cold and selfish," my mother complained. "You'll die alone and friendless like your grandmother" (her widowed mother-in-law, relegated to a dark apartment in the Bronx). The curse, no doubt translated from the Yiddish, almost sounds Italian, in dialect. But then friends can be cruel, too.

The narrator announces that she is finally going to win because she is now solely in charge of "our story," all that remains in her mind, everything she still remembers. The writer is the keeper of memory. And here resides my dilemma. The one who tells the story owns the past, but that story, even shared, becomes one's own; like Elena, you can't help making it up in the process.

I must have over a hundred letters from Naomi, the earliest from 1971. I find them hard to read. It's not just a matter of deciphering her handwriting—that comes after a while, and most of the letters are typed. What's tricky is my knowledge of how fraught my attempt is to tell "our" story without erasing or distorting hers. I want to be fair to Naomi's truth. At the same time, I know this is impossible. All that resides in my mind is mine, although as with Elena's memory of Lila, what I remember includes how Naomi saw me, too.

Except for the letters of 1976-77, for which I kept carbon copies, what remains, with a few exceptions, is a one-way correspondence. This is not to say that I'm not present in the letters. On the contrary, Naomi often replies to questions—or gossip—from my letters to her, and because of her mania for defining our relationship, supplies a portrait of our friendship. My letters to Naomi are stored in her archive, unsealed, at the Pembroke Center Feminist Theory Archive. I could take the train to Providence to read them, just as anyone else might. But will I? I hesitate to make the journey. It would be truer to say that I am afraid. On one hand, I'm afraid of the self I will find there—the person I was, maybe still am; on the other, I see this book as a work of memory, not documentation, even though I have been unable not to borrow from Naomi's letters to me. Her words have become implanted in my mind, jostling memory, becoming memory. What future readers will find in her archive may lead to yet another story, not mine to tell.

Sometimes I think about memory the way I do about yoga props. Yoga teachers urge us to use the props and not consider them a weakness, but rather as an integral part of the practice. I resist leaning against the wall to balance, though I often need to; I resist putting my hands on cork blocks to manage a difficult pose, even though I know this is stupid, that I shouldn't care. The older I get, the more compromised my body, the more limitations undermine my practice, the more I persist in denial, until a teacher walks over and slides a block under my hand, relieving me from my struggle. I doggedly want to rely on memory alone here—without props—and yet I am already compromised. The letters I've read are at work in my brain, reshaping memory.

In *Blue Nights*, the memoir about her daughter's death, Joan Didion writes, "Memories are what you no longer want to remember." The problem, of course, is that that we do. But if you don't retrieve your memories, confront their truth and their lies, you can never mourn. That's what memoir is for.

THE GROUP

One cold, solitary Sunday morning in January 1971, a month
before my thirtieth birthday, I was leafing through the *Times*
magazine when "Consciousness," the title of an article by Vivian
Gornick, caught my eye. I was living alone, almost for the first
time since leaving home. As usual, I found myself adrift between
bad boyfriends, a familiar state since my return from Paris, a
condition that made me wretched enough to start therapy (even
I could see a pattern there). In the stark pen-and-ink drawings
that illustrated the article, one woman was breastfeeding, another
was leaning sultrily, or maybe sullenly, on a typewriter keyboard,
and a third had turned her back on the other two. (In a corner in
the foreground, a man's face was frowning.) None of the women
looked remotely happy.

"Consciousness," it turned out, referred to consciousness-raising
groups, a new phenomenon. Women would meet to analyze their
lives in intimate detail—including their doubts and fears. That part
wasn't hard to understand. What was different was the notion that
you would look at your own history not solely in personal terms
(though obviously your story belonged to you), but also in relation
to other women and other women's experiences.

The dialogues reported in the article seemed to promise an
answer to the baby-versus-book binary suggested by the images, a
dilemma (could you have both?) that obsessed most of my friends,
but especially Naomi and me. It was one of our main topics. Could
a woman have sex, babies, and a career? The only part I seemed
capable of was sex.

Almost before I finished reading, I picked up the phone and
called my friend Hester Eisenstein to see whether she wanted to

start a group of our own. A few days later, Naomi and I traveled uptown to Hester's apartment to plan our first meeting. Hester and Naomi had been graduate school friends at Yale. I knew Hester through a friend from summer camp. We first met in Paris in the 1960s, and she was a witness to my marriage in Geneva. In 1971, Naomi, Hester, and I were all back in New York enmeshed in the various lowly, early stages of academic life at Columbia.

Friendships made in graduate school were not that different from those forged in summer camp—all-girls camps, at least. You belonged to a cohort, you were subjected to common rules, you competed and got rewarded in recognizable ways. You had crushes on some girls, hated others, banded together when you found your best friends. I loved camp, even though the constant comparisons—who was prettier, whose parents were richer, who always won at volleyball, who had the best front crawl in swimming—were sometimes devastating, even corrosive. But the intensity of the group intimacy, as well as the joy, held me in.

In graduate school, the teachers were the counselors minus the sports. Being good in graduate school was like being good at summer camp, only more specialized. You didn't have to be good at everything, just some things; in fact, the very things you did only in graduate school. Of course, unlike my summer camp, graduate school was co-ed, and all the professors, except for one, were men. The women students didn't compete with the handful of men in the program, however; we competed only with each other. That didn't mean we didn't think the male students wouldn't get the best jobs and become the professors—that seemed a given since there were only a handful of women professors in the university—but their lives were different from ours. For one thing, they often had wives, if they were straight, which they occasionally were, or rather, kept hoping they were until their marriages fell apart under the strain of their secret desires.

The first meeting of The Group was held at Hester's apartment on Riverside Drive and 116th Street. The building curved gracefully into the embrace of the river, which you could glimpse from the bedroom window.

It was a Sunday night. Eight of us sat in a circle, friends and friends of friends.

From Hester's diary, shorthand notes about our first meeting in the form of a list:

> Topics for women's group: love, sex, physical appearance.
> Images other people have of us, bullshitting: honesty with
>   our friends.
> Abortion, femininity, aging, motherhood, coming to the
>   group.
> Our mothers, marriage, money.
> Work, competition with women, competition with men.
> Do we exist?

We had all read the *Times* article, so we knew what to say about why we were there. Not knowing what we were doing, or why, and not being satisfied, were themes that echoed. We were mostly in our late twenties, old not to know, we felt. It was as though we were in transition but couldn't see the next step. Were we like each other because we were women or already friends, or because we were fucked up?

⊞ ⊞ ⊞

Hester began by giving her first name and her job. She was running the Experimental College at Barnard, which Kate Millett had
started. We all said our first names and jobs after that, but Naomi,
as if to affirm her attachment to her family, added her last name.
I had been eager to lose that attachment, and getting married had
been a quick way of doing that. My surname still belonged to my
ex-husband, but it felt like a dumb charade to be carrying that identification around with me four years after the marriage had ended.
On the other hand, it provided a shorthand narrative: I had been
married. Now I wasn't. The failed marriage was a kind of badge,
like a botched suicide attempt, which was also in my collection of
unhappiness: a little story of past suffering, with the tiniest hint of
glamour, self-pity transcended. So long ago. My ex-self.

"I'm in graduate school," one woman said, "because I don't know
what else to do." Almost everyone nodded in agreement.

"I wish I were back in graduate school," Naomi announced with
her typical contrarian edge. She had been skeptical about coming
to the meeting: "You know I don't like groups," she had said. "You
don't have to come back if you hate it," I told her.

"At least you knew where you stood," she went on. "And what
you did was validated." "Isn't the job itself validation?" Hester asked
at the meeting. "I mean, a job in an Ivy League school in New York,
with an apartment in the Village?"

"Yes, but what good is having the job if the smartest man in the
department thinks your work is out of date?"

Naomi had a way of eroding sympathy for her position by pushing its negative potential to the extreme. She and I had analyzed
this propensity too many times for me to contradict her in public. I
hoped someone in the circle would say what I couldn't say, or what
Naomi wouldn't hear from me.

I was teaching two sections of beginning French that met every day, but the stipend didn't provide enough money to live on, so I tutored for extra cash. For the entire two hours of the meeting, as The Group talked about wanting to change, I was obsessing about a very young man I had started tutoring. I wondered if he had called and whether he would. And I wasn't thinking just about the French lessons.

That April, we all went to a Town Hall debate that would become famous, between a panel of women intellectuals, notably Germaine Greer, Jill Johnston, Diana Trilling (looking uncomfortable), and Norman Mailer. During the debate, Johnston boldly performed her sexual politics, kissing her lover on stage, cheered on by the audience, ignoring Mailer. "Jill, be a lady," he pleaded limply. Susan Sontag, speaking from the audience, explained to Norman, as she called him, that women did not like being called "lady writers."

⬛ ⬛ ⬛

We imagined ourselves as part of a new kind of history, a history that would be created by telling our stories and documenting them. This was key to the consciousness-raising ethos. Each woman's narrative would illuminate the larger pattern of women's lives, our collective oppression under patriarchy, as we un-self-consciously said. Of course, we were thinking mainly of ourselves, nice, middle-class, mostly Jewish young women (I almost wrote girls), and our stories. It did not occur to us that our "we," which seemed a giant step forward from "I," just as un-self-consciously failed, for the most part, to consider our situation in relation to women beyond our cohort.

I volunteered to take notes for Naomi's turn. We had been friends for over a year, so I knew a lot about her background but had never heard her self-narrative. I saved the notes, twelve pages of single-spaced, yellow legal-pad lined pages, handwritten in purple ink.

Naomi's story began with her parents and the mythology, as she called it, of their past as artists, refugees from Poland who emigrated to New York in 1941, having both lost their families in the Holocaust, and ended with meeting the man she was in love with, Serge Doubrovsky, an academic born in France and, key to the story, a writer. That arc, of which she was fully conscious, was shaped like a circle, an irresistible pattern. Among other things, Doubrovsky, seventeen years her senior, looked uncannily like her father, who had died when Naomi was seventeen. He also shared a Holocaust history. One could see the attraction.

But he also was married, with children, and that part of the story did not play well with The Group. We did not, collectively, or on principle, approve of affairs with married men. What about solidarity with other women?

But Naomi said she didn't care about the other woman. She wanted what she wanted and "went after him." (What's the point of having an Oedipus complex, she quipped, if you don't enact it?)

That was August. Earlier in May, we had confronted Naomi about her decision to spend the fall semester in Paris with the man she was in love with, taking a leave without pay, while she worked on the book she would need to be considered for tenure. "You sound like parents warning a child not to put her hand in the fire," she said, refusing to back down. "I'm ready to take the consequences." As a girl, addicted to reading biographies of famous women, Naomi said she thought she would one day be the "first something." But she seemed to have lost her desire for fame and now found herself in an intellectual identity crisis. Her lover was already famous. Was there room for her to be famous, too?

When the Pembroke Archive celebrated its opening with a display of materials from Naomi's files, I saw that from a young age, Naomi had wanted to become famous; as an eight-year-old, she had saved a check for two dollars and labeled it "my first check for my writing." There were later proofs of prizes and honors, some I hadn't known about. I felt not only less successful but, contrary to her view of me, keenly less ambitious. I could not think of a single moment of longing for recognition or accomplishment or "fame" (certainly not as a child) until I entered graduate school at almost thirty. In the melancholy mood that always underlies the celebration of a life in the absence of the living, it struck me that compared to Naomi, I had led an A- life. It wasn't as if I hadn't already known that, but as I studied the documents in the vitrines, I felt somehow embarrassed for myself.

🞐 🞐 🞐

Hester's diary entries about The Group end in 1978 with The Group's demise. I was shocked to see that I had left The Group several times, though always returning, when what I had remembered was a decade of unbroken fidelity.

I have a way of remembering myself as the good friend, not to mention the good feminist. During The Group's first summer together, we rented a group house on Fire Island. In a photo, four of us are posed like modern pin-ups in various stages of beach undress, sitting on the deck with our backs to the ocean. I'm next to Hester, and we are both looking off to the side at the antics of a dog that one of the women had brought along. My friend Ellen Sweet is looking flirtatiously at the photographer, who was her boyfriend. The photograph moves me as much for how beautifully alive we all look, as for a marker, in black and white, of our early, hope-filled years in feminism.

Three of us are still friends, but while we might occasionally talk intimately, we will never return to that glowing summer ease of young women circling our thirties, tightly bonded. Naomi asked me to send her a copy of this picture. Perhaps we were the image of female comfort that she missed in Paris.

I stare in a kind of wonder at the gigantic head of hair—an Afro wannabe—I paraded around for most of the seventies, almost worthy of Angela Davis or Kathleen Cleaver, I hoped. (What was I thinking?) I note the fact of my flat stomach, the way Nora Ephron remembered the time in her life when she could wear a bikini, the bittersweet backward glance at a body long missing but from photographic records.

Bodies. I also remember that one evening, when the men had returned to the city, the woman with the dog told us about her four abortions and how she thought of each as a child with a name. That staggered my imagination and made me realize that I had never thought of my one abortion as losing a living child. Maybe that failure of imagination underlay my failure later to conceive. In the spirit of feminist truth-telling, we felt compelled to refuse the stigma of abortion, even in the plural, and nodded in sympathy.

THE CARDINAL OF PHILOSOPHY HALL

For most of the 1970s, Naomi's and my conversations and letters circled irresistibly around the most powerful man in the French department at Columbia, Michael Riffaterre. He had changed his first name from Michel to Michael, and intimates called him Mike, which was pretty implausible given his irreducible Frenchness, not that I ever called him by his first name, long or short. We students referred to him as "the Riff" (as in "Reef," or "Rififi," both of which carried a hint of danger). Sometimes in conversation, he vaguely alluded to being Jewish. He probably came from one of those old assimilated French families, but we were never sure. Rumors swirled around him. He was missing part of an earlobe. Some people said he had been injured in a duel, others that he had been a hero of the Resistance. He had also been married before but how many times we did not know.

Riffaterre was a collective obsession. No detail of his behavior went unnoticed or uninterpreted by Naomi and me, particularly the degree to which he did or didn't notice us. Being noticed was the first step to being recognized. We were not Sleeping Beauties. We were awake with expectation. We were waiting for the prince to make his way through the forest to where we were sitting in front of our typewriters. Naomi thought he might have already picked me. Whenever I stared into the pit of insecurity for too long, she'd point out that he was directing my dissertation, even though his century of specialization was Naomi's, not mine. True, I was "good eggs," as he liked to say, mangling idioms when we spoke English, which we usually did. But that wasn't reassurance enough.

No encounter with Riffaterre was too small to report. What he said when we met at the mailboxes; how he looked at our legs at the faculty party; the question he asked the visiting lecturer, humiliating him publicly and making the audience quiver at the sight. "God, he's so brilliant," we junior people sighed, with that little frisson of pleasure produced by a senior scholar's disgrace.

"This is not a charitable institution," the man would invariably respond if you dared complain about his treatment of students. That is what he replied when I had criticized him for mocking a presentation in the Stendhal seminar. The unfortunate student told me that when almost everyone had left the building after class, the Reef waved her into his office to discuss her report and tried to kiss her. The scene was interrupted when the department secretary knocked on the door to tell him he had an important phone call. I asked the student why she didn't report him. "You're not even beautiful," he had said when she protested, nailing the point: "Who would believe you?" She believed him.

That was before the rules on sexual harassment were in place, not that they would have hindered him. Riffaterre was a favorite of the administration.

Because of the rumors about his reputation, it did feel slightly dangerous to hear the door close behind you when you came for his office hour, but the thrill seemed worth it. You never knew what he would say or do, though you knew he'd stop at nothing to have things turn out his way. He looked and acted like Cardinal de Richelieu. Your fellowship would be renewed if you kissed his ring.

⁙ ⁙ ⁙

When I was in his office, he usually answered the phone himself. He called his wife "mon petit," as though speaking to a small child, which I thought was very touching, or at least endearing. While on the phone with his wife, he mostly nodded and spoke in a low, comforting voice. But that didn't prevent him from glancing at me with complicity from behind his desk, distancing himself from the intimacy he seemed to be sharing with his wife. It was as if he were saying that only the two of us knew what really counted: the life of the mind; the mistress, not the wife. Actually, it was hard to tell what the looks meant. Maybe he was talking to his wife in code. She had been his student and was known to say, "My husband is my teacher, and my teacher is my husband." Despite his many betrayals, she always smiled meaningfully when she said it.

One night, midway through the winter departmental party at the chairman's apartment on Riverside Drive, Riffaterre and I stood face to face. Naomi and I always dressed up for these occasions. It wasn't dress to kill, exactly, or even dress for success, depending on the kind of success you were after, naturally. It was more like dress for attention, which wasn't difficult given the standards of academic life, despite the fact that fashion and shopping were respected activities in French departments.

That night I had achieved a look I hoped read attractive, not begging for attention, but hoping to be noticed: a black tunic over matching black pants made out of a slinky fabric that defined the body without clinging to it. What made the outfit, I thought, was a red foulard with black and white circles resembling targets. The scarf redeemed the black from mere starkness and provided a touch of a scarlet identity. Not the red letter but a note of defiance.

I was holding a tumbler of vodka on the rocks in one hand and a cigarette in the other, talking and gesturing as I tried to come up with witty and sarcastic things to say to my advisor. I had my hands full, as it were. Riffaterre stared at me through the thick lenses of his glasses and surveyed me up and down. Then he slowly raised his glass toward his lips and, without smiling, said, "Very nice," while gently grazing my right breast with his knuckles. His eyes never left mine, and I tried to keep mine completely blank. I could feel his wife across the room watching, keeping track. He had turned his back to his wife, but she had memorized his moves through the cloth of his pinstriped suit.

I was determined to show nothing, since to register the gesture would have meant accepting it. By acting as if nothing had happened, nothing would have happened. I took "very nice" as the appraisal of my outfit. "I bought the scarf in Paris this summer," I said. "I thought so," he smiled. I accepted his approval without admitting that the very thing that had conveyed it—his touch—had in fact occurred. The problem was that I couldn't be sure I had won the game. I couldn't be sure he didn't know I was faking it. I suspected that he knew I had felt the touch and that there was nothing I could do about it.

I was caught in his game. Riffaterre controlled our destinies, so I pretended that what was deliberate had been inadvertent. I hated that he could cross the boundary between us whenever he chose to, and that he knew I would let him. "He's dangerous," Naomi always said, knowing his vote would decide her tenure.

But flirtation didn't guarantee a vote. In fact, it usually meant just the opposite. For a woman, being attractive was like being a good teacher for a man. You'd think that being a good teacher was a quality your colleagues would want to reward you for. But Columbia was famous for not tenuring anyone who won the "Best Teacher" award. A beautiful woman, likewise. Beautiful women were good assistant professors. That way, they stayed young. The sort of woman you'd want to keep should resemble a doormat, more or less. (And keep was the word: "Will they keep her or throw her away?") A spinster or a mother. "A working horse," Riffaterre said. Someone you could wear out with the work the men didn't want to do. The gorgeous Ann Douglas, in the English department on the sixth floor of Philosophy Hall, was the exception that proved the rule. They sometimes made mistakes, of course; sometimes the doormats got feisty after tenure. But for sure, you wouldn't want to tenure someone who thought she deserved to be kept. Naomi was beautiful and wore her entitlement like her favorite purple velvet suit. She didn't see why style should be held against her. It worked for Julia Kristeva.

LOVE STORIES

What can you say about a 28-year-old girl living with a married man in Paris? Well, first that her life is very complicated, very interesting and rich. Second that it will probably drive her to the shrink's.

—Naomi to Nancy, December 7, 1971

In September 1971, the letters began from Naomi's first semester in Paris with her married lover, as we thought of him in The Group. A few friends saw them off for their transatlantic crossing on the *France*. It seemed glamorous, if anachronistic, to be traveling by boat, and the *France* was a serious cut above the student ships that had taken us to Europe when we were young. It turned out that Lionel Trilling and his wife were sailing with them; seen from a distance, it appeared that Diana Trilling did most of the talking, Naomi wrote in her shipboard chronicle.

This must have been the first time I met Serge, after having heard about him for over a year. He found me "demure," Naomi reported, using scare quotes and an eye-roll equivalent exclamation point. Also, I had a "very nice back," whatever that meant. No one had ever commented on my back (and no one has since), and the phrase stuck in my memory, mixed in with the grab bag of remarks about my appearance I've collected over the years from French men, who, despite their ostensible desire, never hesitated to appraise the article spread out before them in dispassionate detail. (Serge was nothing if not French.)

Over the summer, I had met the Fencer, as I'll call him, after a James Taylor concert on Martha's Vineyard. He had been a college athlete and still looked the part; he was also a cartoonist for a downtown newspaper. I moved in with him that winter, leaving my studio on the Upper West Side for a funky, ground-floor tenement on Charles Street (still, it was the Village), a block away from Naomi's stylish walk-up on Perry. We were looking forward to being neighbors when she returned from Paris. For the first time since Naomi and I had known each other, we were both trying to write (her tenure book, my dissertation) while living with men we took seriously. The high-stakes challenges of loving someone and getting work done were intertwined and, for Naomi, palpably impossible to disentangle. It's not that it was so easy for me, but at least my boyfriend was not a famous writer or a distinguished academic against whose career and talent I measured myself.

In her first letter from Paris, Naomi composed an "auto-critique" of how living not alone but in a couple, she had forgotten what a "moody bitch" she could be, indeed how like Shakespeare's Kate in *The Taming of the Shrew* she was as she wrestled with her demons (not that Naomi, like Kate, was ever really tamed). The Fencer once accused me of wanting someone outside the door of the room in which I was working only when I decided to emerge, and not a life partner. It's true that most of the time I was more pulled to writing than anything else. I dressed as a typewriter at the first Halloween party we went to together. It was a great costume, but the Fencer was not amused. The next party I went as Valium.

For Naomi and me, our efforts to write in those early years and the unfolding of our love relationships received equal time in our letters. "It's really a struggle," she wrote in response to how I described daily life with the Fencer, "to retain some form of humanity while deeply involved in one's work." In the early days, I hoped that work (writing the dissertation) and play (drinking martinis, watching television, sex) could coexist, if one combined structuralism with feminism (meaning mainly advice from The Group and endless "relationship talks").

I had always been moved by some pursuit of happiness, and I still yearned for the kind of overwhelming love I had fantasized about. But suddenly work, teaching, and especially writing loomed larger than mere happiness. I had begun to see something outside of me—work—as a driving, sustaining force. Naomi had already made that commitment to career when she fell in love with Serge, but that didn't make living the twin desires with him any easier. She saw him as a genius, with work occupying the primordial place in his life. This in turn made her ambivalent about her own work: unsure and insecure when she wanted to be strong and independent. The Fencer was not an academic or even an intellectual, which undermined our analogies at the root, though Naomi and I loved our construct of two women friends living parallel lives.

◫ ◫ ◫

It's easy to see now how Naomi and I failed to take the measure of, though all the while acknowledging, the profound, psychic differences between us; we so much wanted to be in the same story, and of course in many ways we were. Our professional circumstances were bound together; our fate controlled by the same tyrannical man, Riffaterre; our work life subject to the same requirements and the same clock-driven schedule of production in the same institution.

But Naomi was the daughter of artists, who were also European immigrants, and whose home bathed in the radiance of a charismatic father, painter, goldsmith, raconteur. She saw herself, she often said, as the sole uncreative member of a talented family.

In counterpoint to the visible, visual achievement of her father, mother, and sister, it was as if she had nothing to show. What could match their canvases? The stakes of academic accomplishment, intensified by her lover's fame, could not have been higher: "I think Serge will not marry me if I don't write a book! How's that for an incentive!"

I grew up in a second-generation, Jewish American home dominated by an athletic mother with a phenomenal will to power that my father accommodated. I longed to escape their dominion, and it was academia that represented this escape to me. But however different the families we came from and the men with whom we were living, despite the disparity between our places on the ladder we were climbing, we could and did analyze our problems in tandem—as if they were the same; as if we, therefore, were also the same.

For the longest time, insight and our relentless, daily commitment to analyzing our situations and each other, did not propel us out of the maze we had created, because they also formed the glue that held us tight. The confusing, turning pathways of love and work that led us in circles and twisted us in knots were woven into the fabric of our friendship, what Naomi liked to call our mutual aid society-cum-heart fund.

NAOMI MILLER

A few years ago, when I went back to the letters from this era of our friendship, I found, at the top of a pad of yellow draft paper: "A Year in the Life, or The End of Masochism."

Short version: True to my habit (or what was starting to look like a habit), I ended a relationship that had appeared to all as giving me a semblance of bourgeois stability by starting a disastrous love affair with a married man. I left the Fencer and moved into a building on 79th Street and Amsterdam Avenue, where friends were living and, as it turned out, across the street from Naomi's mother. This was the tenth time in fifteen years I had moved, but I would stay at 79th Street for the next fifteen. Thanks to a low building opposite ours, I could see the Empire State Building through the kitchen window. It was a sliver of the kind of view I'd longed for since leaving home, but a sliver that felt more like a slice, especially at night when the lights on the spire changed colors.

I loved the apartment, the first truly grown-up apartment for just me, though I did not love life for just me as much as I thought I would. In some ways, my academic trajectory was on track—I had a prestigious fellowship that in theory left me time to revise my dissertation into a book, the key to my survival in the profession. But whenever I looked at the stack of dissertation pages I had once felt proud of, I either fell asleep at my desk or felt like throwing up and had to lie down. Although I could produce conference talks and articles, it was as though something in me had ground to a halt, as if my anxiety about getting tenure and the next job paralyzed my ability to do the very thing that would be necessary for that to happen. I knew that but seemed incapable of taking action on my own behalf.

You can see why masochism was the flavor of the year.

When I left the Fencer, I hoped that the man I had become obsessed with would spend more time with me. I could never admit, even to Naomi, that I wanted him to divorce, as she had with Serge from the start. I just wanted more, more of him, I would say. But my freedom changed nothing in our pattern, except making it easier to meet. Of course I wanted more than ease.

I did not regret having ended the relationship that had sustained me through graduate school and my baby steps in the profession. I needed an intellectual partner, I came to realize, more than an enjoyable companion, despite our affection for each other. The further I moved ahead in what had started to resemble an academic career, the more frustrated I felt in conversations with the Fencer. I needed something all the charm of a superb raconteur and attractive personality could not provide.

I had not reckoned, though, on how the economy of my newly single life would come to feel more like privation than fulfillment. I could barely afford the rent (which was half my monthly stipend), buying furniture put me in serious credit card debt, and I was stuck with a neurotic, unloving cat a previous boyfriend had foisted on me as a substitute for his affection when he moved out. (In those early feminist days, so-called sensitive men went on so-called trips, leaving the women behind to wait like Penelope.)

Above all, I had a great deal of time to ponder what was wrong with me and to hang on to the crumbs of affection my lover (I'll call him Philippe) was willing to share. Sex, yes; commitment, no. Had I learned nothing from Naomi's relationship with Serge? It seemed as though he'd never leave his wife, never have a child with her; her friends thought Naomi should leave him. So what hope did I have? None, and Philippe made that clear from the start. "I won't take you to Tahiti," he said the first time we slept together. "We're not going to live in a post-structuralist cave." Did that give me pause? Of course not. I smiled.

田 田 田

I have never wanted to admit this, but I don't see how to avoid it, pulling out the thread of perverse attachment, a doubly perverse attachment, that further blurred the boundaries between Naomi and me: Would I, if Naomi hadn't shared her passion so intimately with me, have plunged into my affair with a man, at least by category, like Serge—married, French, older, an academic—thereby destroying a sustaining, if imperfect relationship? Did I somehow want to become closer to her, erasing the space between us by a kind of mimetic involvement, conveniently ignoring the major differences in the men, in us, in the structure? After all, I wasn't mourning a dead father.

I can't avoid now seeing the dangers of the over-identification that ultimately undermined our relationship. Naomi's first book was almost entirely based on René Girard's theory of mediated desire. I have the sinking feeling that I somehow proved his hypothesis, though more abjectly: not just wanting the object of the other's desire (in my case a copy, a first degradation) just *because* the other person wanted it, but wanting to *be* the other person.

At a reception for the visiting scholar Tzvetan Todorov, I reported to Naomi that Riffaterre had steered me with his hand at my elbow to Mary Ann Caws, a senior scholar known for her work on surrealism, who was chatting with the guest of honor. "Have you two met?" he asked Mary Ann. "Oh, yes," she said. "Naomi Miller." She quickly corrected herself (Mary Ann is nothing if not quick), and in fact I had not had the name Nancy Miller for long. I savored the moment, knowing that Naomi would be as pleased as I was by the fusion. "I LOVED Mary Ann Caws's surrealist slip," Naomi replied, "It really says it all."

We loved being two in one, two as one. We needed the doubling. We needed each other, sometimes desperately.

▣ ▣ ▣

There was a best-selling book published in the eighties called *Smart Women, Foolish Choices*. Naomi and I could each have contributed a well-documented chapter titled "Sex and the City," *avant la lettre*. Mine, I admit, would have to be a prime example of the refusal, on the part of a relatively smart woman, to accept the evidence that the adventure she had embarked on was doomed to failure from the start. It quickly became the source of extreme, punishing pain. Throughout the year Naomi was in Paris, I tried to end my affair, mainly by reporting in every letter that I was trying to do just that. Instead, I got rid of Viva the cat, who had begun to systematically destroy my expensive new couch.

As different as the men in our lives were from each other, the problems in some ways remained the same: our moods and our feelings about our partners, our work and each other. Whatever the fluctuations, those were the elements of the configuration and, above all, the state of our bond, which generated running commentary.

A relationship as intense as ours, as "*erotic* (in the broadest sense) as ours," Naomi wrote from Paris early that fall, is bound to have its ups and downs. In the margins, she scribbled that she was upset about everything by way of mitigating the adjective.

A few years later, in one of our more difficult phases, Naomi's sister, Mira, quipped that Naomi and I had the "most intimate, non-sexual relationship" she knew of. "You really should see a therapist together," she wrote, "a sort of friendship counselor." She wasn't wrong.

⊞ ⊞ ⊞

Gail Caldwell describes the power of the attachment to her friend Caroline relatively early in her memoir. Both women are writers, but their shared profession rarely takes center stage in their story:

> Because we had known of each other for a few years before we'd met, we had relied on that implicit assumption between writers of recognizing the other's achievement; in most relationships, this commonality of purpose would more than suffice. But Caroline had never said anything directly about what I did or what she thought about how well I did it, though she had given me a copy of her memoir and asked repeatedly if I had liked it.

Looking back, Gail, who received the 2001 Pulitzer Prize for Criticism (not mentioned in the memoir), links the depth of feeling the friends had begun to have for each other to their identities as writers: "Finally I blurted out, 'I have to ask you something difficult—I need to know what you think of my work.'" Caroline is horrified to realize how her silence weighed on her friend, and as they continue their walk, they talk about writing for the first time, about "what a swampland this was: the world of envy and rivalry and self-doubt (between women, and writers, and women writers), about insecurity and power differentials." (It would be difficult to find a better description of academia.)

Despite the comfort of hearing her work praised, and the relief that follows the confession, Gail is "unnerved" by the acknowledgment of her vulnerability. When Caroline asks what's wrong, Gail replies, " 'Oh no,' and finally, 'I *need* you.' " But the next chapter opens with Caroline's reciprocal avowal: "She would say, I think, that the need was greater on her end."

We don't wish to feel wanting in the category of need. It's a mark of affective symmetry between women friends. At the same time, we don't expect to feel unsettled by its place in our lives.

In the first volume of *Memoirs of a Dutiful Daughter*, Simone de Beauvoir, a writer not given to effusiveness in the matter of emotions, describes the very moment she measured her attachment to the most important friend of her youth, her classmate Elizabeth, known as Zaza. The new school year finds Simone unexpectedly morose, when Zaza approaches her and starts a conversation. As they speak, Simone begins to feel an intense sensation, a shock that overwhelms her nervous system: "That's what was wrong; I needed Zaza!"

> I needed her presence to realize how much I needed her. This was a blinding revelation. All at once, conventions, routines, and the careful categorizing of emotions were swept away and I was overwhelmed by a flood of feeling that had no place in any code. I allowed myself to be uplifted by that wave of joy which went mounting inside me, as violent and fresh as a waterfalling cataract, as naked, beautiful, and bare as a granite cliff.

Beauvoir records the emotional tsunami with hyperbole verging on ecstasy entirely unmediated by the notes of restraint or irony that give the memoir its tone: "Zaza was my best friend: and that was all." They talked, Beauvoir remarks, about everything, except for "girlish confidences." Over the years, the friendship nonetheless becomes girlish enough as the two embark on fraught love stories, but what's remarkable in this account is the tension between the almost sexual, certainly erotic, account of discovering the passion in herself for a friend and the boundaries crossed by the over-whelming power of the feeling that strips her bare.

The power of need to rearrange the inner lives of women friends that Beauvoir describes resembles what Naomi and I felt in the early days about finding each other: "a flood of feeling" that resisted categories. I guess you could call that erotic.

Once, after a stay with Naomi in Paris, I sobbed uncontrolla-bly as I walked down the stairs from her apartment, bumping my suitcase from landing to landing, even though we would be seeing each other in New York soon enough. I feel strange admitting to the feeling even now.

LES PARLEUSES

What we need is a clito-colloque.

—Naomi to Nancy, November 6, 1976

In part because we so often did not live in the same city, our letters are punctuated by a longing to talk and, of course, to know what the other thought of our writing. During the long year of our separation, we both narrated our lives, our struggles with work and with men, in an uninterrupted flow, almost as though we were sending each other diary pages. But we were also trying to figure ourselves out together—what we wanted, who we were becoming. Our friendship was also public in the little world of French departments and MLA conventions in which we performed. It gave us an odd sense of being a couple, a tiny frisson of what, exactly, we hardly knew ourselves, though we felt we were creating something new: women who compete with but also *complete* each other. This required staying even, not just between ourselves, in what we felt for each other, but in the eyes of others. "I feel that in our milieu we are not perceived as balanced," she wrote. "I'm tired of being a wallflower."

We were who we were by comparison, both to each other and, especially as our careers progressed, by how we were seen in our tiny universe. This presented a new, agonizing challenge: What counted as success for each of us, and what did it mean? It seemed there was no one we could trust, least of all Riffaterre. (In this we were correct.) "Your problem is not believing the positive feedback," Naomi decided, "my problem is even more pathetic: feeling I can't ask for the feedback." As always, we were both alike and unalike: That was our bond and our bind.

⊞ ⊞ ⊞

Talking. In the eighties, each of us married, we kept on by phone, long distance. Sandy, impatient with my need to rehearse a problem endlessly, would throw up his impatient husband hands after only the second rehash, and say, "Go call Naomi."

⊞ ⊞ ⊞

Talking. "Talking to you," I write, "makes me feel sane; and it's not because you (sometimes) feel as insane as I do. It is the act, the exchange that stabilizes."

Then, anticipating Naomi's Christmas visit: "I am sick of having paper between us. I can't wait to see you." There was no end of needing to talk:

> I wish we could have a tape recorder—like *Les Parleuses*—not to listen to write/right away [the era of constant bad puns] but for future reference. What do you think? I just think that we are the most interesting people we know, so why should it all disappear. Do you think it pretentious to compare ourselves to Marguerite Duras?

Pretentious or not, we made the tapes that Christmas, and during the spring semester exchanged them in addition to the letters. I've kept the tapes, though I've never been able to listen to them since. I don't think I could bear to hear our voices from that year, especially Naomi's beautifully modulated one, in so much pain as we kept circling the same structures of unhappiness: Would Serge leave his wife? Would I give up on Philippe? Would Naomi publish

her book? Would I revise my dissertation, as Philippe was prod-
ding me to do, and write my tenure book? As the world turned,
our letters featured scripts for the academic soap opera in which
we starred; we wrote them and performed them. "Some day I will
have to Xerox my letters to you," Naomi writes, "as I cannot seem
to keep a journal. Besides, I think I give the best of myself (and the
worst) to you in my letters. . . .Pleasure and memories to store up
for the *troisième âge*."

So here I am in old age with a record of my life for which I have
mainly the pain of nostalgia. We were that year heroines of novels we were unable to write—and our letters unwittingly provided
material for a novel in which Serge made himself hero.

AMBITIOUS WISHES

Mme de Graffigny, I have it on good authority, once said in a
letter: "Je veux être homme."

—Nancy to Naomi, April 5, 1977

C., a French friend visiting New York, was staggered by the
volume of the Sunday *Times* sitting on my coffee table. Did I read all
two hundred pages? she wanted to know. No, but I could not bear
the thought of not having it there to read. "It's the same with men—
for you, both needs are a function of lack," she said. Lack was one
of our biggest subjects as we plunged into the psychoanalytic waters
currently in vogue, and debated all night, as I reported to Naomi
the following day, whether penis and phallus were the same thing.
"I remember your saying," I wrote, "that you didn't so much want to
have Serge as be him." "Serge's mind still turns me on," she answered,
"and that is perhaps my supreme value. In the society we live and
operate in the Phallus that turns me on is a penis with a PhD."

⊞ ⊞ ⊞

Together, we crawled slowly toward an exit from our existential
conundrum. It was as though Naomi, on leave, and I, on fellowship
and reduced teaching, had the leisure not only to torture ourselves
with our failures and inadequacies but also to find a way out of
the emotional morass holding each of us back. Early in the spring
semester, Naomi described coming to the end of a quest, a quest
that had propelled her through her teens and twenties, the death
of a certain romantic ideal, an artifact of her life with Serge. At the
same time, she acknowledged another kind of death, and the cause

of the deepest level of her depression. She had tried several times, she said, to sit down and WRITE. It wasn't happening. "Somewhere I believe like Serge that a life outside of literature is not worth living," she said.

"I want to write a book myself, about myself," Naomi explained. Two years earlier she had described the dream of writing such a book, but a novel, not a memoir, about "the wife/female companion of a would-be creator in such a way that it would not be dismissed as sour grapes." She would call it *Muse*. But the project felt hopeless: She could not move "beyond the nuclear scenario," she said, diagnosing her problem as having had "a father who worked out in the open, and was a total shlemiel at selling himself. And I am no better."

The most unsettling effect of rereading this correspondence is not so much confronting what I remember (which is bad enough), but what I don't. I do not remember Naomi confessing, almost with shame, at having had the dream, now relegated to the status of fantasy, of a literary ambition. Perhaps because it had never been mine; I was still dreaming of becoming an academic. I'm always struck by instances from these early years in which we were out of phase, since in my narrative of how the friendship was built and then collapsed, we did not struggle in the beginning, rather like the conventional retrospective of second-wave feminism. In the beginning, we experienced unchallenged solidarity; eventually the cracks in the white walls of sisterhood became apparent.

There is an astringent effect to retracing these turns. I'm forced to confront the enormous holes in my narrative of our psychic journeys.

Naomi liked to equate her desire for a literary life (fame?) with mine for academic power, a lesser ideal, in her view. But was it power and its politics that fascinated me, as she thought, or my rage at our collective powerlessness as women at a time of economic crisis? Or, less grandly, the simple fact, of which all the assistant professors (not only Naomi and I—I had become an assistant professor in the spring of 1974) were aware, that we were rivals in the economy of scarcity, the logic of which dictated that where one succeeds, the other must fail.

▣ ▣ ▣

In March, Naomi's academic book on Zola was accepted for publication. This was, as she had to admit, great news, but the acceptance came with a caveat: She had to translate all the French quotations into English, which meant that she would have to retype the whole manuscript. That was not a catastrophic requirement, but an annoying one. Either way, she wrote, "I feel nothing even approaching elation or euphoria. I cannot coincide with my joy." There was something "bittersweet about the victory."

I promised to help with the translations. She said she'd thank me for that in the acknowledgements. "I *love* the idea of being acknowledged," I said.

She dedicated the book to Serge and inscribed my copy: "For Nancy—the woman in my life, a palimpsest of thanks. With love, Naomi, December 21, 1978."

In 1977, Serge had published his novel, dedicated to Naomi and his mother and inscribed to me, also with love.

By 1978, Serge and Naomi were no longer together.

The book contract changed everything, since it was the book Naomi needed for tenure, but also, ultimately, for me. "Now it's your turn," she said. So here's how we kept ourselves in the same story: "I'm convinced that one of the reasons you have not sent out your dissertation," Naomi wrote, "is that you are afraid it might be accepted!" True, we preferred our fantasies to what always felt, after the fact, like meager accomplishments.

What did these women want?

⊞ ⊞ ⊞

We never loved the same man, but there was a man whose power over us remained unabated for almost two decades, until I finally broke the spell—or he did: Riffaterre. "I must tell you about a fairly unbelievable conversation I had with Riffaterre," I wrote.

> Thursday, my last day on campus before the break, I felt as if I were dragging myself around. I saw that Riffaterre was in his office, and I had about fifteen minutes before class. I decided to go in. I wasn't at all sure of what I wanted to say, although I know what I wanted from him. I was pretty much on the edge of tears but not in a sentimental way; it was more a kind of bottomless despair. So I walked in and sat down, and after thirty seconds of pleasantries about the party, I asked, "Do you still believe in me?" I hardly said anything after that—except that I was having a failure of nerve and that I sometimes worried about never having another "idea." The rest of the conversation was on his part. (I should say here that I think he was stunned, as was I, by the nakedness of my presentation of self.) He said things that he had said before—that I am a person of substance, top notch, etc. It wasn't so much that that got to me.
>
> What did get to me was more personal: that I had had a big upheaval in my life, he said, that one couldn't always operate at

the same level of productivity, that it wasn't only quantity that counted, that he was a machine but that was his trip (he must have used another word), that he had worried about teasing me too much. And then, that if his life had been arranged differently, he would have "besieged" me with his attentions, that were he to find himself on a desert island, he would enjoy my company and thought I would enjoy his. (I said nothing.) I can't remember everything, but it all seemed momentous at the time. I suppose the conversation had been prepared somewhat by a brief exchange at the party: that he would never forget the first time I shuddered in his class, that he often imagined me curled up in the back seat of a Rolls covered with a courtepointe, etc. (Telescoping the two conversations, Philippe translated: "I would marry you if you had money!")

The crucial thing, I think, is that I didn't ask, and he said nothing, about the future. Had he proffered the rotten carrot, that would have poisoned everything. And that really wasn't the point. For a moment, I thought of asking him if he would help me in the future. But then I thought again: It's like asking someone if they will love you forever. (As Philippe commented, "Daddy came through.")

Do I remember this episode? Not really, though once I had reread my letter, I suddenly saw myself back in Riffaterre's office, as I had been so many times, as a supplicant. Nonetheless, the scene belongs here as an aide-mémoire, if not memory itself, a memorandum of how it was: exactly what I'd prefer not to remember.

▣ ▣ ▣

The Fellows had been invited to present our work at a dinner with the head honcho of the Mellon Society—whom Riffaterre always referred to as Big Daddy. (I was awash in daddies.) I described the event to Naomi in great detail, narrating the scene, and highlighting Riffaterre's reaction to my presentation, at first skeptical, then, seeing the positive response in the room, pleased, finally praising me in public:

> And if I ever had any doubts about his role I can forget
> that too: he is into it. I don't quite understand why I feel
> so re-connected to him now; I guess it's because I'm so
> needy; want so much for someone to take care of me,
> look out for me.
> . . . . I dreamt all night that Philippe was having affairs
> with other women.

(He was.)

I'm retyping my abjection, but what can I say? That was how it was: for me, for Naomi, lived and narrated between us, our shared Oedipus.

"I loved the scene with Riffaterre," Naomi replied. "I'm sure you trouble him and always have. I hope that you were able to measure and savor the impact of your personality. "

My personality. Perhaps the greatest mystery is that one: How can you know what your personality is, since it is completely dependent on how it is perceived and by whom? There's a mirror for beauty, but not for personality.

Do women friends always play on opposites, or was it just the two of us? In part, our comparisons—our sense of self-definition in relation to the other—described who we were in the present tense of friendship. But each of us also operated out of a deep neurotic structure itself based on comparison, invidious comparison in which each of us lost in our own eyes.

◫ ◫ ◫

One of my earliest memories of understanding who I was in the world, how I fit, was the constant contrast with my younger sister. "How is your beautiful sister?" a guest of my parents would ask in guise of a friendly greeting, when I opened the door for company, as I liked to do. Each time, the question, which was actually a pronouncement, felt like a blow that annihilated me. I was not surprised. I knew my sister was beautiful. What I did not understand was why I was supposed to enjoy the fact. In adolescence when I discussed this with my sister, she'd say, "Well, you have ideas, and I don't." I no more valued "having ideas" (whatever they were) than having the fifties alternative to beauty for girls interested in boys: personality. What good was personality?

On a trip to Paris with my friend Jane Opper to celebrate our PhDs and shop, I introduced her to my French friends. The consensus, inevitably reported in the form of a comparison, no more forgiving in French: "Jane, quelle beauté; Nancy, quelle personnalité." I had trained myself to laugh, of course: Jane is the beautiful one. In Naomi's family, she was considered the beautiful one.

I would have liked to have been the beautiful one.

AUTOFICTION

Toward the end of the 1970s, Naomi left Columbia for Brown and broke up with Serge, just when he was finally ready to divorce and even, what he had always refused, contemplating having a child with her. In one of the many maxims that organized the man's world view: You can have whatever you want in your life, but never when you want it. Q.E.D. It had never occurred to him that Naomi might one day stop wanting him.

The first decade of our friendship coincided almost entirely with the span of Naomi and Serge's affair. Our relationship didn't end with theirs, but in some ways Naomi's departure from New York signaled a change in our bond neither of us understood, or even acknowledged at the time. Naomi got an Ivy League job with tenure in a French department—the dream. I got to stay in New York, another one of our dreams, ultimately with tenure, too, but also with full-time administrative responsibilities, running the Women's Studies Program at Barnard. I loved Barnard and felt saved from ignominy by the Women's Studies Program, but it was very much not tenure at Columbia. I continued to teach in Columbia's French department, though without a say and, of course, still in fealty to Riffaterre.

I rode to Providence with Naomi in a van with her belongings. We set up her bookshelves so that her new study mirrored her old. But she was embarking on more than a new job; it was a new life, and our worlds were starting to resemble each other less and less. This would be the first of the knotty moments over the years where we needed to recalibrate the rhythm and intensity of our relationship but somehow didn't. We had survived as "les parleuses" all through the French leaves; why would American miles change anything, especially since we still had "long distance"?

We both knew we had to change. In some ways, our love and need for each other, our passionate attachment, despite the history of our affairs, stood in the way of committing to a life partner. It was easy to forget, hopeless hetero junkies that we were, that we also did want that, however much of a mess we had made in our couples. Naomi said it first, as she tried to console me about the separation. As if to prove her point, almost immediately after establishing herself in Providence, she married Paol, a handsome Breton poet who had fallen madly in love with her at first sight. Two years later, Naomi threw a party for friends who had attended a conference near Providence, and it was there that I met Sandy.

"He's worth getting past the polyester," she said, when I complained about his grungy academic appearance (actually, it was a short-sleeved nylon shirt he'd had since high school), thus sealing the deal.

⊞ ⊞ ⊞

Three years after Naomi left for Brown, Serge published *Un amour de soi*, the title punning on Proust's *Un amour de Swann* (*Swann in Love*). Serge's novel plots the course of his relationship with Naomi ("Rachel" in the book), from their first meeting until the breakup. The last words of *Swann in Love* famously express the anguish of the character's belated discovery (shared by the author, now called Julien) that the woman he had been madly in love with did not, in the final analysis, correspond to his aesthetic ideal: "To think that I've wasted years of my life, that I've longed to die, that I've experienced my greatest love for a woman who didn't appeal to me, who wasn't even my type!" The narrative ends, or appears to end, with the breakup. But the novel itself, constructed as a series of spirals, is followed by a section titled "Coda (In Cauda Venenum)" (as if there weren't already poison enough). It's composed of a series of letters: the first from Julien (the author's character) to Rachel, announcing his divorce, the second from Rachel's mother hoping for a good outcome now that the divorce is final. The rest are from me, "Annie," to Rachel in Paris.

My year of letters to Naomi translated into French.

In the "Coda," Julien describes how his new wife urged him to sort out the boxes piled up in the cellar of the apartment building where he had lived with Rachel over the years of their alternating New York/Paris existence. In a carton of Rachel's abandoned books and papers, he discovers a packet of letters that shed new light on their relationship and on the breakup. Shocked by what he learns about Rachel's feelings for him through the letters from Annie—that she had always been in love with someone else—the author hesitates between suicide and murder and, encouraged by his eager new partner in crime, decides on murder—literary murder, of course. "A woman is like a book," Julien says, contemplating his pocket knife in a meditative passage. "Rachel, I'll bleed [*saigner*] her, I'll mark [*signer*] her." (*Saigner/signer*; the guy never could resist word play.) The novel was written to rid the narrator of Rachel's power over him. As Julien's new wife says in the novel, egging him on, "This way you won't regret her! One always embellishes memory. You see, she never even loved you; it's the other guy, John, she loved." The coda supplies the author's justification for writing the venomous tale that, as readers, we have just swallowed.

I put the book out of my mind for almost twenty years. But when, after Naomi's sudden death, her widower assigned everyone a specific aspect of Naomi's life to recall for the memorial held at Yale, and asked me to revisit the years we were both assistant professors at Columbia, I found myself doing what I vowed I would never do: I reread the novel. I read like an academic, scribbling page references in the back and marking the most disturbing passages with Post-it notes.

Going back over that reading, now, almost another twenty years later, I can see what I took from the novel on that occasion in 2002 and what I missed. What I missed then that hits me now with a different kind of violence, violence surely different from what I must have felt in 1982, a time I have trouble retrieving, except as the delayed, refracted pain of a traumatic wound, is the representation of my friendship with Naomi.

I stopped this time over the novel's depiction of us, Rachel and Annie, Julien's analysis of Rachel as from childhood in need of a double. I was only the latest in this model but irritatingly present in the role:

> The two of them, not a pair, a real couple. To see herself, to understand herself, Rachel doesn't need a mirror, it's a twin. . . . Currently, Annie, number one, the great love. I'm offended. Really, which of us counts more, Annie or me? Some days that annoys me.
>
> —You keep talking about her, always Annie!
> —That's ridiculous, you're jealous?
> —No, but you spend your time looking as if you're going to devour each other, as if you hadn't seen each other for ten years.
> —You don't understand anything about friendship between women, it's different.

(Be my mirror.)

❊ ❊ ❊

1982.

Naomi calls from Providence to tell me about the novel and the letters. Paol had brought the book back from a trip to France. "You won't be happy," she says.

"How could you? How could you leave my letters behind?" I ask. She really has no answer. She didn't realize that she would not be returning. There were so many books she had to bring back. But still, a packet of letters? My letters? *Our* story?

The author no doubt rationalized, even bragged about using my letters in terms of "autofiction," a term he had coined earlier in his career to describe his twist on genre distinctions: taking literary license with a narrative that purports to be the true account of real events. Certainly, using my letters was an extreme case of manipulating the truth in order to tell a good story, and an easy way to solve a literary conundrum: how to justify the hatchet job he performed on a woman he once thought he loved, the proof in black and white.

Proust was not enough.

In France, I had grounds to sue the author for the publication of my letters. But beyond the expense, I would have had to identify myself as the author of the letters in public. To do so, Philippe Lejeune, an expert on autobiography in France, explained to me picturesquely, would complete the author's crime with my own hands. The shameless author would no doubt have enjoyed the publicity. Still, out of solidarity, I would have run the risk if Naomi had decided to sue, but she didn't. She seemed more resigned than horrified. Beyond its tell-all flamboyance, the book was an artifact of literature—the ultimate prestige always for her—and, in a way, however perverted, a tribute to how much the man had loved her. She felt guilty about leaving, falling out of love, loving someone else, and so accepted the ugly portrayal of her as just punishment.

And, besides, the book had done its harm, spread its poison. Beyond the little world of French departments, ordinary readers would have no idea who "Annie" was. But we did. And so did everyone we knew in the Columbia French department, not least Riffaterre who, at a cocktail party at which he and Naomi found themselves in Paris after the breakup, commented that she had inspired a "petit-chef d'oeuvre."

But I did not press my case. I always found it hard to be angry with Naomi, or rather to admit I was angry. I feared her anger, her displeasure. And often I mollified her, as I did my mother, wanting to ward off the violence that might ricochet and come back to wound me. Later, many years later, when we were in full rupture, I said I was tired of placating her. Naomi smiled sadly and said that was one of my best characteristics.

In the process of searching for our correspondence from that year, I came across a letter from Naomi, writing in 1989 about a literary prize Serge had just received for a new novel that narrated the relationship of the author with his second wife, the woman who urged him to use the letters for the Rachel novel. The woman—in life and in the story—killed herself (it's not clear whether she intended to) by combining large amounts of vodka and drugs. On a popular literary television program in France, the author boasted that he killed one woman per book.

The tremendous success of the new book revived Naomi's anger about her portrayal in *Un Amour de soi*, complaining that it was riddled with "lies, distortions, and pathos." The key word here is *distortion* (from the Latin *torquere*, to twist and to torture), a phenomenon harder to get at than an out-and-out lie, and much harder to track (hence the inherent potential for betrayal in autofiction).

But, of course, isn't distortion precisely the *truth* of any relationship, including my own with Naomi?

However uncomfortable, the truth of human relations resides in the fact of relationship—and to say *relation* is to say *relative*. Add memory to the mix, and we quickly see how tentative our confidence in narrating a friendship must be. If any account of the self includes relations with others, how can an autobiographer tell a story without betraying the other, without violating the other's privacy, without exposing vulnerabilities, without doing harm, but nonetheless telling the story from one's own perspective, which, by virtue of being a published text, exerts a certain power? You—the person whose life is being written about—enter willy-nilly into the public domain. Faithfully recorded or maliciously distorted, your story circulates, utterly outside your control.

I can't find a way not to confess my friend while confessing myself. I can't get back at the man without reinjuring the woman. Besides, what is the power of my truth against his fiction? Nothing I can say or write can prevent the novel from existing. And I'm still mad about that.

PENIS/PHALLUS (ENCORE)

At end of the 1980s, as I moved from Barnard and Columbia to CUNY, and from Women's Studies to English, I also turned from writing about French literature and French women writers to a more hybrid, autobiographical criticism. Naomi disliked *Getting Personal*, the title of my new book. "We're not doing the same thing, anymore," she said one day, almost bitterly, as if I had somehow violated the terms of our friendship. She was disappointed in me, and I felt stung by her disdain. I swallowed my hurt, tried to defend myself. After all, we were both still academics, feminist critics, still had read what we had read and loved, dissected our relationships, measured our masochisms, compared our depressions. But books were in no way objects outside of us; they were always an essential part of our story. Perversely, then, our books, which had been at the heart of our parallel-lives pact, "united by friendship," became "scattered by discord," in another of Cicero's metaphors.

My embrace of autobiographical criticism, however, was neither strictly literary nor solely tied to my leaving a French department, though it was academic. In my last semester at Barnard in the fall of 1987, Riffaterre invited me to participate in a fancy summer institute where I would teach a seminar on feminist criticism or, better yet, "carry the flag." (He had a mania for American clichés.) I was, naturally, flattered. The requirement of the teachers, beyond the seminars, was to circulate new work to the community, work that would then be discussed in public, with Riffaterre in the role of respondent. I had just finished an experimental essay about feminism and was looking forward, nervously, to the discussion.

The day of the presentation, Riffaterre and I were both seated on stage, facing the rather large audience, including all the students of the school. His response, which he read out in a sullen mono-tone, was not about the specifics of my paper or argument. Rather, he took bitterly against Feminist Criticism (his capital letters) for "othering" him, telling him "our" books were off limits to him (so much for my carrying the flag). When it was my turn to respond, I said I wouldn't because his critique had nothing to do with the work. I was, in fact, stunned into muteness. I could not fathom how this man, my advisor, supposedly also my mentor, a man who claimed to admire me, could deliberately humiliate me in a public space to which he had invited me. But then, he could not fathom why, after the event, I refused to "break bread" with him, why I had not just risen to the bait on stage and put on a show to entertain the audience.

That summer I wrote "My Father's Penis," an essay that I placed as the final chapter to *Getting Personal*, and that emerged from the combined strain of taking care of my father who was suffering from Parkinson's disease (he would die the following year) and my public shaming by the man Naomi and I believed was the ultimate judge of our work.

Riffaterre and I never spoke again.

So, yes, Naomi and I were no longer doing the same thing, because I could no longer believe in the phallus, as we used to say.

DEPRESSION

In the early nineties, as I was finishing a run around the reservoir in Central Park, listening to Carole King sing "You've Got a Friend," I burst into tears. Friendship wasn't working its magic. I wasn't sure I could be a good friend to Naomi or that she could help me emerge from my black hole. I felt lonely. For the first time, I began taking antidepressants and reluctantly went back into therapy, even doing a stretch on the couch.

Neither of us was happy in our lives. We often talked late into the night about our frustrations with work—our writing, our jobs, and everything else. We criticized the husbands and their children, and we criticized colleagues and friends, in unremittingly negative language. We regularly succumbed to tangles of envy. It seemed as if we had played our last cards and felt we had been dealt—that we had dealt ourselves—losing hands.

When Naomi married Paol, she spent summers at his house in Brittany, which did not suit her, despite the beauty of the landscape. The climate seemed to aggravate her struggles with writing, her sense of isolation and purposelessness, a version of the depression that plagued both of us at different times. In my response to her account of life in Brittany, I do not seem to have been a sympathetic friend and, instead of comfort, offered suggestions for changing her attitude.

If ever I needed persuading of the selective quality of memory, of the ease with which I've managed in places not only to gloss over but in effect delete whole chunks of emotional history, this letter would do it. I am forced to confront Naomi's narrative according to which I proposed myself as the standard bearer of psychic balance and self-improvement: Be more like me. The debate of whether we were alike continued that summer with what felt like higher stakes.

Wanting the other person to change. Yes, I'm sure my husband would agree with that analysis.

Even so, my problem with this portrait is that I do not remember myself as someone to inspire admiration. In the summer of 1993, I remember trying to start a new book with as much self-doubt and insecurity as ever. I cannot imagine suggesting, even implying, that Naomi become more like me. I struggle to see myself in her words, so blind, so uncaring, so deaf to the pain she was describing. I am wounded, in retrospect, by this indictment, and belatedly even sadder than I had already been at having failed to be the friend she needed. The portrait has one merit, though: It proves my theory about friendship, albeit in its saddest version. Naomi saw me as I would love to have seen myself—competent, successful, moving forward—rather than the cowering, miserable creature I felt myself to be, a view honed from my childhood.

This was also the beginning of my fear that her depression would keep me tethered to my own. I was desperate to move out of our mutual misery narrative and into another story. I sometimes feared that my fragile composure would fall apart under the weight of Naomi's despair. But I also could not imagine my life without Naomi. Esther Perel, a couples' therapist Sandy and I were seeing during this difficult period (we had our own problems), said that it was one thing to separate from someone, another to separate from the feeling driving the separation in oneself. I sensed that was true, but it seemed easier to break than to penetrate the heart of wretchedness in myself.

How does one separate from a friend, a friend like oneself?

Naomi wrote an academic essay on psychic suffering called "Depression in the Nineties," which was included as the endpiece to a collection of literary essays she published in 1995. *Bad Objects: Essays Popular and Unpopular* is the only book of hers that I bought (we were no longer speaking, but I still wanted to know what she was thinking) and that she didn't sign for me.

Trying now to put the pieces of our separation back together, I'm surprised to see that I was still connected to her in the book, through the preface, dated fall 1994, the year before our breakup, as a reader of the manuscript version. And here, which I also did not remember, Naomi reluctantly puts a toe in the water of the autobiographical criticism she had rejected in my work earlier. "Clearly," she acknowledges, "it is time for me to get personal, more personal than I have ever been in print, which isn't very." What led her to become a "critic of nineteenth-century French fiction and . . . a somewhat contrarian feminist theorist"? It's above all her beginnings as the daughter of Jewish Polish immigrants, artists, whose last country of residence in Europe was France, their complex linguistic legacy, including Yiddish, her schooling at the Lycée Français, and her academic career.

But in "Depression in the Nineties," while Naomi notes her "melancholic disposition," she diagnoses "depression as a condition internal to academia," not a matter for Prozac or Zoloft. More specifically, in the essay's incarnation as an MLA talk, she associated her personal depression with the changing status of feminist criticism: "We, the now middle-aged feminist critics of the seventies and eighties, have simultaneously lost the two pillars of feminist criticism as we knew it: narrative and gender."

Between 1994—when I listened to the MLA talk—and fall 1995, my depression had become a kind of irritability, even rage. I don't doubt that a certain professional frustration dogged us both, aggravating whatever suffering was already in place. In 1995, I was struggling with a book that wasn't thematically feminist, but, perhaps reflecting one of Naomi's passions, more "universal," dealing with the death of parents, not uniquely by gender. In the course of one of our phone conversations about the book, Naomi said, "Well, maybe you're not a writer." A real writer—Flaubert, Proust, the man she had been in love with. Maybe I wasn't a writer. I did not take the thought well. Since rediscovering Naomi's poignant confession from two decades earlier, her soul-crushing admission at discovering she wasn't the writer she dreamed she might become, I've begun to wonder if she was also saying, "Maybe, *like me*, you're not really a writer."

▦ ▦ ▦

In the final volume of Ferrante's quartet, Elena frets, "Now that I'm close to the most painful part of our story, I want to seek on the page a balance between her and me that in life I couldn't find even between myself and me." I, too, have been trying to find that balance. I want to be fair, but I can't see myself clearly, except as myself seeing Naomi and being seen by her. I can't escape her vision of me (Elena's problem as well). I have reams of her words about me, but I can't be sure whether I was that person, whether she was the person I wrote to, or whether I coincide with the portrait she created, the image that I had both absorbed and denied.

Letters: hers, mine; lost and found.

▦ ▦ ▦

In the summer of 1995, I taught a seminar that was surprisingly well paid. I decided to splurge on a few days at a fancy fitness resort in Arizona. Naomi and I had been to spas before, once in France, once in California, with intense pleasure at our luck being together far from home, with hours to talk into the night. That winter I could not imagine wanting to share the experience of being in the desert landscape I already knew I loved, indulging in spa luxury, and then having dinner, sinking into gloom as the sun set. I also could not imagine how to tell Naomi I was going without her. I bought my tickets and, as the departure date grew closer, stalled almost to the day, until the words burst out of me.

In an email I told her that I was going to make the trip alone. I'm not sure exactly how I put it. But whatever I said, and however I said it, it delivered a blow the force of which I had neither measured nor intended. Our mutual friend Jane Gallop reported that Naomi said she was hurt when I announced my plans but that I didn't seem to care, that I was in fact angry: "That, after years of sympathizing with her suffering, you felt there was no place for your feelings in your relation to her." That part seems true. But what I should have done about that if I wanted to preserve our friendship is another matter. Part of our pact was the commitment to bearing each other's pain. What Naomi would not see was that her suffering had become hard to bear and that she felt entitled to its primacy in our relationship. How could I be angry with her when she was in pain? She had endured mine. I was angry at not being allowed to be angry.

But, of course, Naomi was angry, too, since in her view, my anxiety about the depression only masked deeper, uglier feelings: "resentment, competitiveness, and envy." It's painful to type those words; it's even more painful to triage the truth more than two decades later. Her depression, my resentment. Yes. I envied her Ivy League privileges. I had not reckoned, when I left Barnard and Columbia—willingly!—on what the lack of amenities and resources at a public university would mean: no research budget, no significant travel funds, no merit raises.

As the exchange went on, in one brutal envoi after another, her depression and my resentment became hopelessly entangled. At that point, we should have stopped emailing, picked up the phone, met, and talked. But it was early days with email, and neither of us realized how dangerous a mode of communication it could be: letting feelings fly across the internet, uncensored, deaf to the possibility of harm. Letters had allowed us to paper over the cracks that had opened between us; email exposed them.

It's as though, to return to the metaphor of the double face, the double-sidedness of friendship, we had allowed the strains of the B-side to mute the harmonies of the A-side.

RESTITUTION

"We'll see who wins this time," Elena crows in the prologue to Ferrante's quartet, but what is winning, exactly, when you've lost your most intimate friend? Getting to tell the story. In the epilogue, titled "Restitution," Elena announces, "I've finished this story that I thought would never end." Lila has disappeared from the life they shared and withdrawn from all contact, with no explanation. The friendship ended with a rupture, possibly caused by *A Friendship*, a new book in which Elena recreates the narrative of what it had meant for the two to be girls together. The book sold well and revived her literary reputation, but Lila refused to talk with Elena about it and wouldn't say why. "So I had to acknowledge," Elena concludes in the fourth and final volume, "that our friendship was over."

What, then, might we understand by *restitution*? Toni Morrison ends on the sadness of an irretrievable past in *Sula*, a novel in many ways like Ferrante's about the intertwined workings of memory and female friendship. Nel speaks in the aftermath of her friend's death, years after their estrangement: " 'We was girls together,' she said as though explaining something. 'O Lord, Sula,' she cried, 'girl, girl, girlgirlgirl.' It was a fine cry—loud and long—but it had no bottom and it had no top, just circles and circles of sorrow." Reflecting on creating *Sula*, in the essay "The Site of Memory," Morrison recalls the way her mother's friends talked about a certain woman, which led her to think about "friendship between women. What is it that they forgive each other for? And what is it that is unforgivable in the world of women."

◨ ◨ ◨

In the five years of our estrangement, Naomi and I had intermittent contact. We acknowledged each other's birthdays (do you know how hard it is to forget a birthday you've remembered for years?), and we sometimes saw each other at professional meetings, where our rift was known, making for awkward public encounters, especially with friends who tried not to take sides. We met for coffee once or twice at Edgar's Café on the Upper West Side when Naomi was in New York visiting her family and exchanged the odd email about an event that affected us both. But starting over for good, the way we had been, seemed hopeless. Was it even a good idea? I apologized, though, the next to last time we met and cried. Naomi took my hand in sympathy. But it was not forgiveness. The saddest thing about our breakup was that I had not intended to initiate a total rupture. True, I desperately needed us both to end our long, dismal conversations of complaint about our lives, exchanges that left me flattened. I wasn't sure I could see a way out of our pattern, but I wanted at least to change the conversation about it. Instead, Naomi took my frustration as a full-scale rejection of the friendship. She quickly escalated what might have been a difficult moment into an ultimatum: Change or it's over between us. And I let that happen. But as awful as it felt, there was also some relief. I never stopped thinking about Naomi, about what had been "us," but once we entered the "it's over" territory, I felt that she had to want some kind of renewal for me to make an overture. I did not know what I wanted or imagined, but I longed to exit from the stupidity of our rupture.

▨ ▨ ▨

In 2001, a few days after 9/11, Naomi came to New York for a party her sister Mira was giving at her studio in Chinatown. I had been walking around downtown, taking snapshots, as many people were, of the mutilated landscape created by the attacks on the World Trade Center. I was still holding my camera when I looked up and saw Naomi come through the door, wearing a bright red silk tunic with a mandarin collar. She was smiling broadly, and I captured the momentary radiance that lit up her face. We made a date for coffee a few days later and returned to Edgar's, scene of an earlier fiasco.

⊞ ⊞ ⊞

Here's what I remember about our last encounter. It was strange to be together again, but also familiar. We were circling in and out of time, the women we had been, the people we were now, or wanting to be. There was no face, no smile I wanted to see more. Naturally, we spoke about work, almost immediately. Naomi was trying to write a book about universalism, the theme that had engaged her imagination for several years. It was not going well, she felt. She had married, a second time, a well-known and prolific critic of French literature. They had married during the years of our not speaking, and I knew little about their relationship. He would have a cup of coffee with her in the morning, she said, then climb the stairs to his study to write yet another five hundred pages. She would sit and read the newspaper, drinking coffee, waiting to want to write. He received prestigious invitations abroad she thought should also have come to her. I could hear our old resentments worming their way into the conversation—hers toward him, mine toward her. I hadn't had those invitations, either.

I had, of course, felt the frustration and anxiety she described: Did anything we did matter anymore? We had lost that seventies conviction of being part of the zeitgeist, our zeitgeist as feminist literary critics. And that was always the pull: I know how you feel. In fact, I knew the feeling so well that I feared rejoining it through her. Would the demon of despair redouble its effects if we resumed our conversation, exposing our worst fears, the beat of self-doubt, the lack of acknowledgment, always heard just beneath the surface of what seemed to be a modicum of success? After all, we were not complete failures, even if something seemed always out of reach, something shimmering over there on the horizon, the glittering prizes going to someone else.

We were starting over, tentatively, taking first steps on the path back to each other, as we had been, and forward to whom we might yet become, together. Perhaps *restitution* is also Morrison's word for the puzzle of forgiveness, for seeing the unforgivable, for recognizing, belatedly, whatever we may have missed in the other, including, of course, in oneself.

A few days later, in an email from New Haven, Naomi wrote, "I've been shot in the heart." She went on to describe her pain at being left out of a footnote in an essay by a historian we both knew. At the end of his essay, the historian had added a long footnote, naming the scholars in French studies he felt were doing significant work.

"But who cares about him?" I asked. "He's not even in literature." That I had not heard of the essay was no consolation to Naomi, either. Nor was the possibility that the omission was an unfortunate oversight. After all, Naomi had just invited the man to a conference she had organized at Yale; he knew perfectly well who she was. Nothing made sense, but I had to agree that the lapse was unforgivable.

⊞ ⊞ ⊞

I could not help thinking: A footnote killed Naomi.

That was not a good way to die.

⊞ ⊞ ⊞

It was a little after Thanksgiving. We were having dinner with friends when Mira called to say that Naomi had been rushed to the hospital. She had been complaining of headaches for a week, and finally the pain became intense enough to require immediate medical attention. It turned out that the headaches were the sign of a cerebral hemorrhage. Naomi had been taking a blood thinner since a liver illness in 1992, a drug that required regular monitoring. In November 2001, with the press of the holiday, she had skipped her last visit. The assault to the brain was so severe that she died soon after being admitted to the hospital; nothing could be done.

I was grateful that Mira had called with the news, as though I were someone who still mattered, who would want to know. I was thankful that the two of us had mended our friendship enough, enough to feel the visceral tug of reattachment, the what-ifs and might-have-beens with heart-splitting violence. How could I have let a moment of emotional lassitude morph into a breach?

The shock of the phone call came back to me two years later when I got the news that Carolyn had killed herself. That ring fractures your world.

⊞ ⊞ ⊞

I don't want to die thinking I've been left out of a footnote, excluded and erased, though it's not a feeling alien to me; alternately, I don't want to be relegated to a footnote, which at best is what happens to most academic work.

At the funeral in Providence, friends and colleagues stood in the chilly rain, listening to the eulogies, crowded together for warmth under our umbrellas. Naomi's husband began by telling us that Naomi used to say no one would come to her funeral. It was a large gathering. We all laughed. That was so Naomi.

▨ ▨ ▨

This was the first time I had lost a friend. She was fifty-eight, which while not a tragically young age, is young enough to feel untimely. I was unprepared for her death, despite the fact she had been close to death a decade earlier. Jacques Derrida, a critic Naomi considered a friend, wrote extensively about friendship. He followed the ancients but also highlighted the implicit vulnerability in the model of the pair: "One always leaves before the other." Married couples can't help knowing this—it's in the vows, after all—but friends rarely consider that outcome when tying the friendship knot. That truth, perhaps obvious only after one reaches a certain age and accumulates a significant number of losses, was true for Derrida. It was the beginning for me.

Diane Middlebrook

We follow a long corridor of words

Till we arrive at the bright salons of fact. . . .

—Diane Middlebrook, "Story of My Life"

3
Diane

FRIENDSHIP AFTER SIXTY

It was 1999. Late-life friends, I liked to say, when I told people about our beginnings. We were both giving talks on the ethics of life writing at a conference in Laramie, Wyoming, where neither of us had ever been. We were about the same height, with short hair and glasses, but no one would have mistaken one for the other or thought we were related. Diane had straight, spiky hair, then a dark auburn; mine curled tightly into a gray topiary. She was distinctly thinner than I was, too, even before her illness, and the shape of her face more angular. But more important than the difference in our respective *rondeurs* (and hair) were our public styles of self-presentation.

On the day of her keynote, Diane strode up to the platform (she was known for her leggy, loping walk and for wearing one red and one black shoe) in a short, form-fitting, bright red leather jacket that flattered her slender figure, radiating confidence, commanding the stage. She was poise incarnate, and her prose sparked fire. If our styles were punctuation, I played the question mark to Diane's exclamation point. Our bond was not about opposites attracting, though; it was almost entirely about the novelty, something like erotic excitement, of two women forming a friendship with decades of stories behind us. But what language, really, is there to describe a friendship between two straight women who, in the photograph from the event, are posed sitting close to each other, side by side, at the conference book table, badged with our institutional names, and grinning like co-conspirators, with our recent books propped up in front of us?

It was a little late to be starting out, but much later than we knew.

In the moment, in the rugged gorgeousness of the Wyoming landscape, what drew me in was the unexpected sound of a new voice, public and intimate, that spoke my language. Diane was completing a dual biography of Sylvia Plath and Ted Hughes she was calling *Her Husband*. And in part because of the difficulties she had encountered with each poet's estate—the frustrating business of extracting permissions from the respective gate-keeping heirs—she made a defiant statement early in her talk about the ethics of biography that startled the audience. "The dead," she announced crisply, "have no wishes; they only have wills." Diane's bold claim shocked many at the conference, but it rang true to me. What else am I doing here but sketching biographies of my dead friends without their permission?

The year after we met, Diane was diagnosed with liposarcoma, a rare cancer that develops in fat cells in soft tissue. Diane's tumor was in her abdomen. There is treatment, primarily surgery, but usually no cure once the cancer has spread.

Diane thought she might outwit the disease.

❦ ❦ ❦

Six years later, as I sat in her living room in San Francisco, look-ing out at the Golden Gate Bridge, on a sunny weekend morning, Diane surprised me with a pair of shoes. "Here," she said, holding up a pair of strappy, red, faux alligator, high-heeled pumps. "I raised half a million dollars for Stanford in these. I can't wear them any-more. I want you to."

❦ ❦ ❦

That afternoon we went to a fancy garden party at the lavish home of friends in the Berkeley Hills. The shoes fit perfectly (how did she know?), and I wore them without teetering, a drink in hand, for several hours. I felt ridiculous but pleasurably tall. Taller. Tower-ing. Followed by a week of shin splints.

❦ ❦ ❦

The plan for the following day entailed bra shopping at Neiman Marcus in Union Square. In addition to the stents that were bothering the lower part of her body, other stents were poking out of her rib cage. She needed a bra that would work around them. We gathered a few possibilities and disappeared into one of the dressing rooms. As Diane adjusted her breasts inside each bra, I watched her evaluate the fit with calm, as if studying her body, mapped by surgery scars, almost dispassionately. She looked at herself with the confidence of a beautiful woman, despite the ravages to her body caused by the illness. She concentrated on finding the right bra.

▨ ▨ ▨

I should not have been surprised by Diane's equanimity when faced with the dramatic transformation of her body. An email from April two years earlier describes how Diane experienced the changes:

> So I guess what I need is a recognizable image of myself
> in this new form, physical and emotional. It's odd, I don't
> actually dislike the shape of my body right now, scars,
> swelling and all; it's just that I don't know who it is, yet.

Who it is.

Who: an image of herself with which to negotiate, adapting her wardrobe to the metamorphosis, almost bemused by the challenge of dealing with a new, transitional self.

Never less than lucid and pragmatic, Diane narrates an inventory of what's hanging in her closet, describing each item with the brio of a magazine writer, itemizing things she can't bear to give away because they are just too beautiful and just might still work.

> A Steve Fabrikant sale item from the late 1980s, a white-
> and-black knit suit with a beautiful shapeliness and a sort
> of thready look—cunningly tattered in the manner featured
> this morning in the InStyle snapshots of women in the
> streets of New York. Hey!

Hey, what do you think of that? "Cunningly tattered" and still in style.

In a meditative pause, she looks back at the lovingly detailed account of her wardrobe, explaining what motivates her analysis:

> I suppose one reason I am laying all this emphasis on
> clothes is that I don't yet really know what I look like.
> My ankles and thighs have re-emerged from their swollen
> state, and the swelling on my surgery keeps changing shape
> in a general downward direction, but I haven't been able
> to figure out what looks best on me.

Diane's "yet" is a hopeful survivor's deferral. Style, not despair.

Not long after my visit, Diane described, in one of her layered messages, an excursion with her son-in-law in San Francisco, providing details of her lunch menu (a loaf of defrosted walnut bread with "fabulous" cream cheese) and recalling our shopping excursion:

> I was, of course, wearing the camisole bra that you bought
> for me. I thought of you a lot, and how much it meant to me
> that you made this trip. It was wonderful to have you with
> me those days. You are excellent company, always. But it
> seems I had a sort of hollow place that you found and filled,
> as well. (No wonder I ate so much of that bread!)

▨ ▨ ▨

Diane possessed the art of making her friends feel loved and appreciated. It felt natural, even enjoyable, for me to be the one flying around, voting, as a lover once snarkily said about his visits to me, with my feet. She made the role easy for me to play, not least because she was generous with her affection, unabashedly kissy with her signature "smooches." And she was also always specific in her language about who you were to her and why: here the bra, the bread and its metaphor of a hollow place. She found my hollow place, too, of course. Especially after the deaths of Naomi and Carolyn, Diane took up the place of "The Friend," the one I loved and trusted to know me, the friend who was also a writer and saw me through my writing struggles. Most of all, with Diane, however briefly, I was the friend I wanted to be. Now that place is hollow again.

⊞ ⊞ ⊞

I haven't worn the red shoes since the fancy garden party in the Berkeley Hills. I was invited to another extravagant party there in 2010, with Diane's daughter Leah, when we were working together on the archives in Diane's study. I knew the party was on our dance card for the weekend, and I thought about packing the shoes in my suitcase, but it seemed wrong, false, as though I had integrated the loss of Diane more fully than I had, and could mourn her by wearing an emblem of her vitality. It still felt too soon, untimely. I hung onto my melancholy rumination, remembering Diane when she was still optimistic, thinking of the conversations we would never have, the walks along Regent's Canal we would not take again.

My inherited red shoes, Diane's improbable gift, have become doubled in my imagination with the doomed ballet slippers of the famed movie *The Red Shoes*. I doubt that I'll wear them again, even though they still fit, but I can't seem to give them away, either.

✸ ✸ ✸

In *The Year of Magical Thinking*, Joan Didion describes sorting through her husband's clothing:

> I stopped at the door to the room.
>   I could not give away the rest of his shoes.
>   I stood there for a moment, then realized why: he would need shoes if he was to return.

It's not that I fantasize about Diane returning, and anyway, these are not the shoes she'd wear in her post-surgery, sensible-shoes reincarnation, but giving them away would be like closing a door I want to remain open. I'm not hopeful, of course, or in doubt of her disappearance. But I prefer to keep her spirit present. I like to visit the shoes that now sit high up on a closet shelf, more than ten years later.

A PAL OF MY DESK

Diane's *Anne Sexton: A Biography* made a big splash in 1991: It was a finalist for the National Book Award. Part of the book's best-selling success derived from the controversial fact that Sexton's psychiatrist, Dr. Martin Orne, authorized the release of tapes from several years of therapy sessions, treatment that ultimately led to Sexton's remarkable emergence as a poet. Sexton won the Pulitzer Prize in 1967 for her collection *Live or Die*, and committed suicide in 1974, at age forty-five. In October 1980, Diane Middlebrook, who had been invited by Anne Sexton's daughter, Linda Gray Sexton, to write her mother's biography, interviewed Sexton's great friend Maxine Kumin at her home in New Hampshire. The book's reception launched Diane's career as a biographer. The two journeys are not without their parallels.

The story of Sexton's beginnings as a poet had been celebrated in "A Friendship Remembered," an essay Kumin published in 1978, just a few years after Sexton's death. "As the world knows," she wrote, describing the relationship between the two women, "we were intimate friends and professional allies. Early on in our friendship, indeed as soon as we began to share poems, we began to share them on the telephone." The image of the friends composing poetry over a telephone line captured Diane's imagination:

> After Sexton built herself a new study, they both had special phones installed at their desks and used them through the day to check out drafts of poems. "We sometimes connected with a phone call and kept the line linked for hours at a stretch," Kumin remembered. "We whistled into the receiver for each other when we were ready to resume."

While Leah and I were sorting Diane's papers—a task we had postponed for almost three years—we found the transcripts of the interview. Kumin had clearly decided that Diane was the right person to undertake her friend's biography, and sounded open and trusting throughout their conversation.

While I recognized some of the exchange from its transformation in the book, I was especially captivated both by the intimate tone of the conversation and by the style of Diane's personality as an interviewer. I could almost hear her voice in the questions she asked and in her reactions to Kumin's answers. The unedited, typed pages, preserved in a three-ring binder, carried the material traces, as it were, of Diane's debut as a biographer, punctuated by her distinctive, calligraphic, handwritten notes. They moved me, sending me back in time, as if through a wormhole, to a Diane I had not known, to the era of typewriters and corded telephones.

To read the interview was almost to feel Diane thinking as she created the story she wanted to tell, picking up the clues she would follow and threads she would highlight in the biography. (I stopped over an intriguing marginal notation, "Mother . . . desk," about the role Sexton's mother played as the family intellectual who had convinced Anne that she was too stupid to accomplish anything.) "USE" in dark ink appears next to a question Diane asked early in the interview about the origins of the friendship between the two poets: "Isn't it true that the John Holmes workshop was the first criticism either of you'd had of work, and that was at the beginning for each other." Diane doesn't wait for Kumin's answer: "I really envy that; I know what you mean, what it must have been like to have someone working as hard as you were on writing." Kumin picks up Diane's thought: "And I miss that! I miss the kind of ongoing, complete encouragement of whatever piece I pick up, whatever comes to my hand."

In a 1968 interview, Sexton recalls her encounter with Kumin at the poetry workshop: "I met Maxine Kumin, the poet and novelist, at that class. She is my closest friend. She is part superego, part sister, as well as a pal of my desk." The interviewer remarks that Sexton once said she called "Maxine Kumin every other line." Sexton clarifies: "I call her draft by draft."

I could not help thinking that Diane's excitement about the collaboration also revealed something about what friendship between women had meant to Diane in her own life as a writer. "I really envy that. I know what you mean."

❦ ❦ ❦

The model of two women working together over an open phone line appealed to the journalists Ellen Goodman and Patricia O'Brien, who, in their 2000 best-selling *I Know Just What You Mean* identify with Kumin's portrait of the friendship: "On that second line, they validated each other's work and life." It was the combination of mutual support as writers with the homely details of domestic life in the course of the sometimes day-long phone calls that captured their imagination: "Interrupting poem-talk to stir the spaghetti sauce, switch the laundry, or try out a new image on the typewriter."

In "Unmet Friends," an autobiographical essay devoted to Kumin, Carolyn confesses to envying the combination of work and intimacy braided together on a daily basis that might have mitigated her solitude in the academy: "Kumin had companions in poetry while I was an assistant professor longing for the sort of world Kumin had discovered and of which I would learn only later, a world of martinis, and fellow poet Anne Sexton on the other end of a telephone line." Kumin represented the epitome of what Carolyn called an "unmet friend," someone encountered only through reading but closer to her than "many friends personally known," and a contemporary. She names their commonalities—a long marriage, three children, the love of animals (notably horses). (They were both also Jewish, though Carolyn doesn't mention that.) Looking back from the renewed loneliness of her sixties in retirement, she wonders, would they, born a year apart, have become friends if they had had the opportunity? Perhaps not. Carolyn remembers herself at Wellesley as being "awkward, considered intellectual and probably off-putting (an impression confirmed by my refusal to wear my glasses, without which I could barely see two feet in front of me and recognized no one)." Even in fantasy, she realizes the meeting probably would not have come off. Kumin had hoped to become an Olympic swimmer; Carolyn confesses to having hated swimming.

Because the interview evoked so much, so movingly, about women's friendship, I wanted to publish it. I wrote to Maxine Kumin for permission to quote from her conversation with Diane. I took advantage of being in touch to ask whether she and Carolyn had ever met. I was especially curious because I had stumbled on Kumin's memoir, *Inside the Halo and Beyond: The Anatomy of a Recovery*, only to discover that Carolyn had blurbed it. What did Kumin think of Carolyn? They met for a drink in the Village, she said. Carolyn sounded very much a professor, and seemed depressed. Carolyn never mentioned the encounter to me, so I have no idea what she made of finally meeting the unmet friend. It was too late to begin a friendship, I'd guess, given her mood in those years.

Envy is one of those pernicious feelings that can erode friendships, contrary to best intentions. But the responses to the open phone line story—Diane's, Carolyn's, Goodman and O'Brien's—suggest that it's also possible to enjoy the fantasy of what other women have and identify with its pleasures in their own story.

Which brings me back to Diane and her friendships (note the plural).

In the hospital during Diane's difficult last days, I met a young friend of Diane's, Kate Moses, a neighbor from San Francisco and a novelist. Kate and I collaborated at Diane's bedside in the hospital, and later by email, trying, somehow, despite the glaring implausibility of our effort, to rearrange the fragments of the Ovid biography that Diane remained passionately attached to during the worst moments of her illness.

After Diane's death, Kate published a remembrance, "Chocolate Cake for Diane," that nailed a quality that I had not quite managed to define myself, capturing Diane's friendship performance with particular elegance.

> Diane's genius was for friendship, a magnetic empathy and curiosity imbued with such confidence in the dreams and aspirations of others that you felt smarter and more talented and more capable in her presence. Talking to Diane carried with it the thrill of a new love affair, of feeling locked into another person whose every word you hung on, and who, you knew, wasn't just listening blandly but in her mind was already erecting the scaffolding for your desires. . . . Diane's critical ingenuity was part of her genius with other people, her ability not merely to believe in you but also

to wrestle your ideas and fantasies into clothes they looked good in. Diane was a stylish dresser.

In Kate's deft metaphor, she also dressed our ideas.

▨ ▨ ▨

Kate met Diane around the same time I did and described the years of their relationship from its inception until Diane's death. Kate had started to imagine a novel about Sylvia Plath and the *Ariel* poems, she recalls, when she discovered in a news story that Diane was working on a book about Plath and Hughes. She emailed Diane, and their friendship took off from the first meeting in Diane's office at Stanford, talking shop and sharing research for the next three years, as well as a passion for Ted and Sylvia. "Our partnership," Kate writes, was "both practical and pleasurable, built on trust as well as pragmatism." Because the two women were neighbors, they had proximity as well as email in the place of the open phone line. Their exchange of ideas flourished and nourished each other—including over cake and tea—much as the phone marathons between the two poets had nourished them. After Diane published *Her Husband* and Kate her novel *Wintering*, the bond between the two women only solidified as they took their books on the road.

▨ ▨ ▨

I had forgotten about Kate's beautiful essay, but I was glad to find it within my Diane files, which included the annotated pages of the Ovid manuscript the two of us had elaborated. It helped me relive those hospital days, as well as fill in some of the chronology of the stages of Diane's illness, the surgery dates I had failed to track. I wanted to return to that moment in the hospital, to fix it in my mind, even though the description of Diane's suffering was difficult to read. But as grateful as I was to have Kate's memory of that time, grateful was not the only feeling the story she told in the essay produced in me.

I was flat out jealous, jealous of *their* friendship.

In an interview in 1975, the year after Sexton's death, when asked about her ties with contemporary poets, Kumin first described her connection to Sexton, "a close personal friend" and "closest contact," but also mentioned William Meredith as an "important pal of my desk." I was astonished to find Kumin using Sexton's expression to refer to her relationship with another poet.

Another friendship lesson learned. There could be more than one pal in one's life, especially in one's writing life.

⊞ ⊞ ⊞

When I return to my emails with Diane, I'm almost shocked by the artful way she does not let her cancer narratives, with their often harrowing details of physical suffering, overwhelm the messages, most of which are focused on getting the writing done, or not. Two interwoven threads between us: the failure of certain cancer treatments, the failure of my agent to place my Paris memoir. The disparity did not bother Diane. We were both writers, even though she was also seriously ill.

So, for example, in a message from the summer of 2005: "Being in work mode myself, I was very captivated by your progress report." Captivated? And, in reference to my obsessively detailed account of all the changes I was undertaking in the hope of making the memoir marketable: "It's so interesting to think about revising work—you have to have a grasp of what seems to be an actual sort of layering in the prose. I like blow-by-blow descriptions of this, so if it's useful to write them, do send them."

In the same message, Diane described a lunch at Oxford in which she and Lyndall Gordon talked about genre and sent me to specific passages in her *Shared Lives* (a memoir I already admired). She found their conversation about writing "useful," Diane said, and explained what she meant by the word: "I said 'useful' somewhat heedlessly here, but it's a feature of my friendship with her, and with you (and also with Carole and Hilary), that they feel *developmental* in significant ways." (Diane and Gordon, along with Carole Angier and Hilary Spurling, created a kind of biographers' club in which they shared work.)

In *Shared Lives*, an elegiac but also political memoir about the group of girls, three close friends, with whom she grew up in South Africa (all of whom died early), Gordon describes one of the three, Romy, in language similar to Kate's vision of Diane. "Could any act of reciprocity give back to Romy" what Romy had done for her friends? "She invented her friends, made us up, endowed us with qualities that were congenial to her. This was the source of her attraction. She gave to each what each most needed." The friend we love is the friend who transforms us into the person we want to be, and consoles us for thinking we're not that person, yet. Diane was a great consoler.

Here's where the ancients' friendship model falls short again, unless we press harder on the metaphor of the second self. The special friend, we've seen, is an idealized figure, which makes the attachment a form of doubling. If the perfect friend mirrors you, then you are exactly like her, also in no need of change, and there's nothing new in the reflection. What Gordon remembers was her beloved friend's ability to *invent* a second self beyond the seduction of the mirror, to create a self that each of the two needs: a reciprocal relation, not a replication. The one, the many, the singular, and the serial.

Carolyn's suicide occurred the day after Naomi's birthday, and revived, if that's an appropriate word, my sense of loss: the loss of my first reader, and then my second. After all, at the heart of my story with Naomi was the reciprocal push to do the work, the writing that we hoped would keep us in the academic world we had chosen. That was the tortured plot line of the transformational year of our correspondence in the mid-seventies, the year, not of magical, but of wishful, hopeful thinking, urging each other on.

Carolyn's unwavering belief in me had also moved me beyond my default position of discouragement, making me acknowledge that I was finally writing my own life (as she liked to put it). Diane became my third reader, inviting me to become a pal of her desk.

▣ ▣ ▣

In 2006, Diane was consumed by her passion for Ovid. I was wrestling with my Jewish memoir, my quest to locate the vanished side of my family, which I was slowly piecing together from scraps and ephemera in the absence of any inherited stories. "I'm so pleased to be partnering you in this way," she wrote, as we compared notes. The belief in craft and recognizing the distinctive challenges of genre and form were central to Diane's credo as a writer. Early on, Diane told me she could never write autobiography—too personal for her taste; I replied that I could never write biography—too long, too factual. Of course, neither statement was completely true. But it seemed important to distinguish ourselves from each other on the grounds of genre. Diane, for instance, was fascinated by a particular plot she called "fictional": how a person from unremarkable circumstances becomes remarkable through artistic accomplishment. This was a bright thread in all three of her published biographies. In Ovid's case, it meant leaving the provincial town of Sulmo as a very young man to fulfill his destiny in Rome; for Sexton, it meant creating herself as a prize-winning poet out of the housewife role and psychic suffering that provided her with autobiographical material. The arc of this narrative of transformation was equally true of Diane, who wrote her first poem at age eight and navigated her way out of small-town Spokane, Washington, to become a star professor at Stanford and a much admired biographer. She told her story, as she of course knew, secreted within the biography of another, undercover.

Diane's back-and-forth with me about our books sounds very much like the collaboration she had with Kate Moses when they were immersed in the Plath/Hughes world. In both cases, Diane could find a way to bridge the gap between very different projects and make the connection meaningful. I began to wonder whether Diane's preferred writing mode found its roots in the well-known collaboration between Kumin and Sexton. No, I think that's exactly backward: Diane looked to Kumin and Sexton for what she herself wanted, needed, and already practiced, and so sought what she knew she'd find.

THE CLINE OF PERSON

Immediately after saying how much she missed Sexton, Kumin adds, "but I feel I was lucky to have her. It was a kind of . . . unbelievable friendship."

Diane presses on: "Anne talked to you about everything, right?"

Yes, and that was a lot of the fun in the relationship. We had absolutely no secrets from each other. I never had a sister, so she was my sister in a wonderful way. It was such fun! I think we were never jealous of each other's careers; of course, we were careful not to compete. We were two very different poets. And we were very careful not to meddle with each other's psyche, but only to try to bring out the best, to be careful crafts people.

"Well, that's a fantastic thing," Diane nods in agreement.

Perhaps what led Kumin to characterize her friendship with Sexton as "unbelievable" was her insistence that it was not marred by competition: "We were never jealous of each other's careers; of course, we were careful not to compete."

The careful decision not to compete ("Of course," Kumin says). Not competing but rather maintaining differences—"We were very different poets"—would be the condition of the highly productive rapport between the two, a connection that allowed for nurturing the writing process while sustaining the bond of love and friendship. How to avoid competition in friendship when two women are writers? I glimpsed the feeling in my time with Diane.

"I never had a sister, so she was my sister in a wonderful way."

Friends as sisters, a vexing conundrum. The linguist Deborah Tannen investigates the sister/friend paradigm in *You Were Always*

Mom's Favorite: Sisters in Conversation Throughout Their Lives. Sisters, she argues, whatever the depth of their connection to each other, inevitably exist in a condition of competition. She goes further to claim that the rivalry between sisters "symbolically . . . represent[s] the universal human dynamic, competition." I admire the feminist confidence that makes the relation between sisters stand in for a human universal (hats off), but I resist the line she draws distinguishing sisters from friends: "A friend might stop being your friend, but a sister can't stop being your sister." While it's true that you cannot lop off a branch of the family tree, a relationship between sisters can end, if not in theory, then in practice.

And yet for many women, intense female friendship is often described as sisterhood, as it so often has been among feminists, when it carries the force of shared history and the weight of necessity. So that when Kumin says of Sexton, "I never had a sister, so she was my sister in a wonderful way," she sounds like a woman Tannen quotes in the book as saying "Friends are the sisters we were meant to have."

Diane doesn't challenge Kumin on the fusion of friend and sister, but she also doesn't let go of the matter of competition between the two poets: "You would leave the phone open and talk to each other while you were writing, and try things out. . . . Well, it must have been tremendously difficult to keep from writing her poem, and vice versa." Kumin displaces the question by emphasizing how different the two poets were from each other in their temperaments: "I was a much more reserved person than Anne, and Anne, of course, was flamboyant and exhibitionistic." Diane then adds craft to personality, completing her vision of how the two worked together. She imagines Anne saying "Does this sound good? Does this sound like me?" Kumin picks up the move: "Does this image work? Does this poem end here? Where should this poem end? Can I begin like this? What about these rhymes?"

Can craft and emotional style solve the problem of competition? "We were careful not to compete. We were very different poets."

Difference offers a hedge against competition. Put another way, the right amount of difference provides the distance to foreclose the drama of competition.

"I never had a sister, so she was my sister in a wonderful way. It was such fun!" In the biography, Diane reports Sexton's version of their tie: "Max and I say we love each other like sisters—that's kind of a new category [for me]. With her blood sisters she experienced only rivalry, but with Kumin, she knew reciprocity" (Lyndall Gordon's word again). Keeping reciprocity free of rivalry, may be friendship's paramount task.

⊞ ⊞ ⊞

What, then, might be the right distance to allow the recognition of difference to be effective and productive? The measurement depends on what Tannen calls "the cline of person," a grammar of distinction expressed in the pronouns *I* and *you* and other pairs like *close* and *distant*. Close and distant, however, "are not on/off characteristics but points on a continuum," rather than being fixed firmly at opposite poles. There has to be some distance for the cline of pronouns—I and you, I and she, or she and she—not to collapse into each other. For to say distance is also to say balance: staying even, not tipping over into gross polarity but rather movement in relation.

Cline as a standalone is an odd word, but I'm persuaded by its resonance. Maybe it's more appealing as part of inclination: what inclines a person toward a particular liking. In French, *inclination* can also mean a move toward love, progress toward deeper connection, often involuntary; we might think in English of the opposite, disinclination, or the falling away of incline.

Tannen's initial mapping of sister relations aligns with the twin poles of ideal connection and competition. She invokes a term used by psychologists for substituting the wrong word for the right one. That's called creating "ugly sisters," as in Cinderella's sisters, who, Tannen points out, were not ugly at all but rather, in the Brothers Grimm original, beautiful. What cline might avoid is casting a comparison that requires one sister to be beautiful and the other not.

Tannen returns to the "cline" story in *You're the Only One I Can Tell: Inside the Language of Women's Friendships*, reflecting on the question of determining how we are similar and different, and what that tells us about friendship. Friendship, she writes, is "a back and forth, a continual negotiation and renegotiation, of sameness and difference," only to conclude that "all our explanations about why we are friends . . . are just ways of trying to make sense of something that has nothing at all to do with reason." Which brings us full circle to Montaigne's "because."

◼ ◼ ◼

In the course of the Kumin interview, the matter of boundaries and resemblance between the two women gets expressed playfully in the matter of clothing.

"We were more or less the same dress size," Kumin recalls, "and one of the joys of our relationship was the ease with which we traded dresses back and forth, and shoes, and pocketbooks, and coats—you know, we really only needed one outfit between the two of us, but Anne was very stylish, and I was very dowdy." Diane seems fascinated by this aspect of their relationship and Kumin satisfies her curiosity with details:

> But we had dresses that we practically fought over: "It's my turn." "No, it's *my* turn." We had a red and white polyester dress back when drip-drys were just coming in to style that we both adored, that we traded—and then at one point we both had the same dress and we wore them together like little Bobbsey Twins.

In the biography, Diane includes that reminiscence about shared clothing, commenting in a parenthetical aside: "(The striking ways in which they doubled each other left a strong impression; today, many people remember them as going everywhere together, though in fact they only rarely gave joint poetry readings and almost never traveled together.)"

They might wear the same things, but one was stylish and one was dowdy. It's safe to make that distinction, if like Kumin you assign dowdiness to yourself. Carolyn did that with me. Naomi and Diane were more stylish than I was, more dramatic in taste and showier in the cut and color of their clothing (I must have looked dowdy by comparison). In the last picture I took of Naomi, she was wearing red. I don't usually wear red, but, in addition to the red shoes, Leah gave me her mother's beautiful red, raw silk, Armani jacket. It's a size too small for me, but I love the jacket too much not to take it out of the closet to wear on special occasions (without quite closing the buttons).

⌗ ⌗ ⌗

Throughout the interview, Diane sounds determined to pursue the thread of possible difficulty in their intimacy, from the fun (one of Kumin's favorite terms for time with Sexton) they had trading outfits to the dynamic of care and nurture Kumin describes. It's as if she wants to know whether there was a cost to the friendship, something that was less than wonderful. Deeply aware of Sexton's psychiatric difficulties, Diane pushes Kumin on the balance in the relation: Wasn't Sexton demanding?

Kumin replies,

> She was very demanding, but I never felt manipulated by her . . . I guess that I loved her so much I couldn't have felt any manipulation . . . There were times that I felt the pressures of the demands, but you know, Annie gave as good as she got. She was extremely generous and giving, loving.

Demanding but not manipulative. Where and how do you draw the line between the two affects? Kumin's own generosity comes through in her conviction that Sexton's need for a high level of care was the former and not the latter. But it is not always possible to maintain the distinction. Sometimes emotional styles within a friendship become unmanageable over time. The power of the other's needs often undermines a friendship. Elena Ferrante's Lila and Lenù, Naomi and me. The cline itself requires care, adjustment.

Miss that moment and the friendship suffers a decline, a fracture, sometimes a permanent one. Does even the "unbelievable" friendship have its limits?

Inevitably, Diane asks Kumin about Sexton's suicide, whether it could have been avoided: "Really, there was no other avenue for her; she had exhausted everything . . . and she had exhausted her friends pretty clearly."

"But not you," Diane continues.

> No, not me. We were still very close, but she felt, I think, very much that I had pulled back from her. And you must remember that by then, you see, I had a little fame to deal with in my own life: I had won the Pulitzer; I was doing a lot more readings; I was in a lot more demand; I was traveling a lot more, and I was not just physically as available to her as I had been. And I think although she certainly did not take it as a betrayal on my part, she certainly felt some small alienation.

Whether Sexton felt put off by Kumin's increasing success, as Kumin imagines (Sexton herself was intoxicated by celebrity), she began to have doubts about the writing.

> She felt that the poems had fallen, and they had. I remember her saying that day when we looked at that last poem, "The Green Room," "I don't know about this poem . . . I think this is just a therapeutic poem." And I remember saying, "Well, it's not a great poem, Anne, but what the hell, there are things in it that are valuable." . . . Because I couldn't lie and say, "Oh, you're wrong, this is. . . ." I couldn't. We didn't have that kind of relationship.

Diane marvels: "She actually was still working on things, and you still had these transactions to the very end, to the day of her death?"

Yes, to the very end.

Transaction, an especially apt term for an exchange, a reciprocity that can flourish between writers who dare run the risk of truth telling in the face of death. There is something beautiful in the power of work, of writing, including criticism, to hold a friendship together, for friendship to expand to contain the critique of writing. But, of course, neither love nor work, nor even friendship, can truly conquer all when suicide is on the agenda: Sexton was only "on loan to poetry, as it were," Kumin acknowledges at the end of "A Friendship Remembered." "We always knew it would end," she concludes. "We just didn't know when or exactly how."

In "Unmet Friends," her essay about Kumin, Carolyn moves from a reflection on Sexton's suicide to the suicide of a friend, the suicide of another that caused her sorrow, not her own. Looking at the essay now, however, it's impossible not to make the leap to Carolyn's identification. For at least a decade, her friends knew Carolyn considered herself to be "on loan." (She used the expression "borrowed time" to describe her late-life economy.) But, like Sexton's friends, we didn't know when or exactly how.

THINKING LIKE A BIOGRAPHER

> ... January draws this bright
> Line down the new page I take to write.
>
> —James Merrill, *The Book of Ephraim*

Diane loved the beginning of a new year, seeing it as the harbinger of new energy for her writing, and she liked to quote those lines of James Merrill, lines that would later appear on the invitation to her memorial service.

2006: One bitter, gray Paris morning in January, I waited outside in the cold for almost half an hour to see the show at the Grand Palais titled "Mélancholie: Génie et Folie en Occident." An exhibit with my name on it, at least the first part. From the Greeks to the moderns, artists represented depression in all its guises and disguises, with many of the early works imagining melancholy through the four humors. When I left the show, I felt a strange lightness. Somehow, despite the obvious discrepancy between a modern, depressed, elderly woman and a history of geniuses, this felt like sublime consolation. In late life, I have come to believe in temperament, in the humors, despite their unscientific status. I'm melancholic, borderline choleric—all that yellow bile making me envious and resentful beside Diane's resilient sanguine. This helped her remain lucid about the evolution of her illness, even as she recognized its severity.

Diane was scheduled for a third lengthy abdominal surgery to debulk her tumor; that is, to remove as much of it as possible. Debulking, an inevitably incomplete procedure (the term of art is "suboptimal"), nonetheless achieves some relief for the patient, alleviating the pressure the tumor is placing on organs. We cancer patients have trouble refusing treatments that might, however finitely, prolong our lives.

Above all, Diane wanted time to complete the Ovid book. She was, in that sense, looking forward to the surgery despite the miserable recovery she knew would follow. To do nothing was also to suffer, and she was never anything but game. *Game* might seem a crude term to apply to the perspective of a long, painful surgery, but it's how Diane dealt with her cancer. If a procedure or treatment with no track record might help even a little, she would do it. This included some dodgy-sounding experiments that her friends feared would benefit the researcher more than the patient, but Diane embraced the gamble until the very end.

That's how it was for her. Diane, I often thought, willed herself into a state of positive toleration, though it might not have been so much an effort of the will as a function of temperament—or perhaps both:

I think it's going to be hard, though. However—thinking like a biographer—I find it somewhat interesting to be passing through this phase of rocks and hard places. Frankly, I think—no, I know—my life is over if this surgery isn't very, very successful. As a memoirist I am sure this interests you too. What if you have good reason to think that you are coming to the end of your own story??? It's a kind of unusual position to be in.

I do not remember what I felt reading this remarkable message. I had not yet received my diagnosis and marveled at my friend's equanimity: contemplating the end of one's life as the end of one's story and finding it interesting as a genre. Interesting! I imagine that I tried then, as the memoirist Diane saw me as, to wrestle my way to an answer on her terms. But now that I, too, have good reason to think I am coming to the end of my life, I guess I would say this book is a kind of answer.

Thinking like a biographer.

Here's what in Diane made our friendship what it was. In the face of imminent tragedy, Diane transformed her physical suffering and what it signified almost immediately into a meditation on writing, but writing as our shared destiny. What do I think about the current debate over memoir and its truth status? She moved us up, both of us, to the plane of writing, to what defined her beyond her illness, despite it. It was a kind of high-wire act that required not looking down. We never really spoke about the end, until it was a matter of months, a time beyond hope. And I managed to be surprised when it came.

I was then, and am even more in memory now, thrilled by the way Diane cast our friendship in literary terms, the open-ended graph of our dialogue, despite the pressures and pains of the cancer on her body:

> Here's a conversation that I hope goes on more or less forever Nancy! I hope you get some good writing time in while I'm out of reach, and also have some interesting conversations with Elaine M., and look forward to a gossip about it all, as my reward for, well, everything, and as an aspect of the good luck that somehow brought us together for just this kind of talk.

The daily prevails through the catastrophe.

Luck. "I could not believe my luck," Kumin said about Sexton. My luck to have had those few writing years with Diane. Of course, as I've said, I was not her only pal of the desk. That's one of the strange lessons of late life. In a friendship dyad you—I—can feel unique, the one. And yet, there always are others. Diane's gift to me.

PAL OF MY DESK (BIS)

2007 October 5

To be honest, I am not very sanguine, and have started
thinking about my will. I need to appoint a literary executor
to handle whatever business is generated after my death.
Would you be willing to do this for me?

I do not intend to place my personal papers in my
estate—letters, diaries, etc.—and have already given away
the archives of the Sexton, Tipton, Hughes/Plath materials. The only leftovers will be my Ovid chapters. I am
thinking that if I can finish this current chapter on Ovid's
Grand Tour, I could make it into a little book titled "The
Young Ovid," or some such. Anyway, I don't think that the
executor's role would be a burdensome or time-consuming
activity, and if you are willing, I think you would be the
ideal executor.

But please be candid if anything about this suggestion
puts you off.

⌗ ⌗ ⌗

If I was startled by the request, it was not least because it came
with the admission that the experimental treatments and ardu-
ous surgeries had not succeeded in arresting the progress of the
cancer. I knew, of course, that Diane had been suffering, but she
typically downplayed the pain in her letters as something that
could ultimately be managed, no matter how awful she was feeling.

She would describe the effects of the illness quite specifically, the pain so "excruciating" at times that she had to take morphine to dull the effects. But in the total shape of the message (her messages were always shapely), Diane never allowed illness to crowd out the complexities of writing, seeing friends, theater going—or shopping, definitely shopping. Put another way, the details of the cancer were almost always interwoven, if not balanced out, with food reports (eating was a major concern given her difficulty ingesting, on the one hand, and the pleasure of dinner parties, on the other), not to mention good gossip from her active social life in London.

⊞ ⊞ ⊞

In June 2007, six months before her death, Diane combined in a characteristic single narrative, work, party, theater going, cancer, and finally, good news about her daughter's career, in complete, punctuated sentences, defying the shortcuts of email:

> I'm just settling down for what I hope will be a productive after-noon of work on my Ovid chapter. I've had the ingredients in my head for a while so I'm hoping the setting down comes more easily than usual. For the past several days have been working on party arrangements, of course—I'll attach the list.

Like a beloved friend, Ovid sustained her throughout the illness, until the very end.

Diane and her friend Elaine Showalter spent summers in London, and the annual summer party, held at Diane's elegant apartment, was an occasion for both women to integrate American and British friends, not to mention a few literary celebrities. It was almost as though despite the illness, life followed its London rhythms: work on the book, party planning, the current theater season. The glissade from topic to topic in a single message, as though they could have equal weight, was part of her epistolary style: Despite everything, I'm still here, I'm still me. Briefly, though, before closing, Diane acknowledges a less than sunny mood: "I suspect that my generally sour outlook comes from ongoing discomfort with my ureter stents. When I'm next in Aschaffenburg I'm going to discuss this with the surgeon and the urologist." She traveled often to a private clinic in Germany for surgery and experimental treatments, undaunted by the growing evidence that little or no success in arresting the progress of the disease had resulted from these stays in the dark forests.

Looking back, I'm struck by how rarely Diane associated difficult moods with the illness, how rarely she labeled and shared them as such:

> And part of the problem may just be my cancer. I don't have as much energy as I remember myself having and sometimes literally have to go to bed around 3 or 4 p.m.: cancer fatigue? If we've been out late the preceding evening the problem is especially acute. Grutch, grutch.

Six years in, Diane wonders about cancer fatigue, expecting, somehow, to be able to remain herself, despite the attack on her body, the diminution of her physical being: "Wish you were here! I'd propose a Monday walk around the garden to debrief on the party."

"Grutch, grutch" (an expression I had to look up).

Six months before her death, Diane signed off with her trademark mark of affection: "Smooches."

Diane's resistance to admitting just how ill she was, her confidence in her doctors and their hopeful views, and her understated, prosey metaphors, made me believe, along with her, that somehow, and against all odds and appearances, she would continue to live. I went along with the narrative, whose lines were clear. I took my job as friend not to get out ahead with skepticism or my anxiety about her future.

A few days prior to the discussion of her will, Diane notes an "an acidy traffic jam" in her esophagus—after which vomiting "clears things out." This latest development, she explains, "really puts a crimp in my communications." She then moves on to describe an excursion to the theater in some detail, "despite the fact that my gas tank feels about empty." The final turn, always managed with grace, addresses the cancer: "The only good thing about this awful illness is that it reconfirms my belief that art really matters. I'm hoping to get back to Ovid this week, even today."

When she was too ill to write, she would reread her beloved Ovid, whose life she had deciphered through his poetry, her companion in bodily metamorphosis. Ovid, *even today*.

I had been planning to visit Diane in San Francisco again in January of the following year, but the "not very sanguine" message advanced the calendar. I traveled instead to London at Thanksgiving. I was to stay in her study—an independent flat on a different floor—and devote my time to reviewing the manuscript with her to see how she might wrest a small book from the original project.

Diane lived in an elegant townhouse in an area known as Little Venice. The house was situated on a crescent, Warrington Crescent, to be exact, a lovely row of identical white Regency buildings, across the street from where Alan Turing, we were told, had lived, and not far from Regent's Canal, where Diane and I sometimes walked. The apartment's terrace looked out over a garden privately shared with the other residents of the crescent. (Having access to a keyed garden is necessary for a truly upscale London experience. Hers was.)

The Warrington Crescent tube stop, however, was located less perfectly, not in zone 1 but in zone 2, thus outside the absolute center of London. But as Diane liked to point out, they were on the best tube line—the newly constructed, sleek Jubilee line—which took her wherever she needed to go in town. The London flat was a fitting counterpart to her apartment in San Francisco, with its spectacular wraparound views of the bridges spanning the bay and the ocean.

◫ ◫ ◫

When I arrived at Warrington Crescent, I was appalled by the changes wrought in Diane's appearance since the summer. She seemed a greatly reduced version of herself, almost skeletal, an already thin person who had become cancer thin. When we hugged, I could feel the bones of her rib cage, the knobs at the top of her spine. Her face, while still recognizable in its angles and planes, now drained of all color, was almost gray. I don't remember exactly what she was wearing—a jacket, no doubt, to cover the lymph-filled belly she had developed after treatment, over narrow black pants. An elegant, fragile shadow of the woman I knew, but still herself.

Despite the unmistakable look of a terminal cancer patient, Diane insisted on fulfilling her hostess role, serving me a snack before sending me back down to her study where I could crash.

Later that afternoon, she ushered me into the living room, where she had served tea, and sat me down opposite her on the pair of facing black leather couches. The doctors had asked her, she said, to decide how and where she wanted to spend the last days of her life. There was nothing more they could do for her; it seemed likely that she soon would need a feeding tube since her digestive system was shutting down, strangled by the tumor. She wanted to return home to San Francisco, she said, to be near Leah.

I want to render this moment more fully, but I feel as paralyzed now as I did then. It's not that I don't remember. I do. I was mute then, mute now. To look at the face of someone you love and hear those words almost exceeds feeling. You hear the words, you know their meaning, and at the same time, you resist letting the meaning expand inside you. Clichés rush in to seal the gap. How can that be? I thought Dr. E. anticipated another surgery?

She's not crying, so you can't. Instead, you sit there and drink your tea like a moron. You begin to mourn your friend in silence.

▨ ▨ ▨

The next morning, we sat at the dining room table overlooking the garden, working side by side. "Side by side" was one of Diane's favorite metaphors for whatever work we did together—editing each other or batting ideas back and forth. This time, all metaphors became literal. We set about to work as if we were embarking on a realistic project: creating a publishable manuscript to deliver to her editor in New York. What I like about Diane's "side by side" as a useful friendship trope is the way the expression suggests a factor of two but two that coexist on the same plane at the same time in alignment. The two need each other.

Together, we would look at Diane's printed-out computer pages. I would then make handwritten notes toward revision on a yellow legal pad, outlining the big picture, salvaging what we could, bringing the bones of the argument into greater relief so that the story could move forward. She would in turn extract the kernels of the changes as she saw them and jot them down in her own elegant script before transposing them to the computer. This kind of editorial revision might even have been enjoyable, and in a way it was, diving together into the heart of the Ovid story as Diane had conceived it—if only, which was impossible—if only she had not been so hopelessly diminished. We did not acknowledge that we had succumbed to a *folie à deux*.

I never asked the obvious: What did she want to happen with the manuscript if she didn't have the time or strength to finish *Young Ovid*, the new little book we were crafting? We never, in fact, discussed how she envisioned my role as executor in relation to the ultimate fate of the book after her death, and I could not bring myself to say, "Well, what should we do with the Ovid 'leftovers' [as she had put it in her email] after you die?" I could not make those words come out of my mouth, nor did Diane say what she wanted me to do. We were paralyzed by uncertainty about how much time remained, but even more so, animated by the fantasy of completion. Despite the evidence that she knew she was nearing the end, unable to eat, we carried on.

I had come as her friend, not her executor. She did not want me to ask.

On my last evening in London, despite her pain and fatigue, Diane organized a small dinner party. Eight guests sat around the dining room table while our hostess presided at the head of the table, sitting straight in the chair, as she always did, barely sipping water. The rest of us tucked in to the local Lebanese takeout she favored, as if there was nothing strange, though it felt like a scene from a Buñuel movie.

I left the next day, planning to continue with Ovid online. I found an email when I returned to New York. Diane had started back to work on the manuscript, picking up where we left off:

> I have already started tracking through your handwriting on the yellow pages in order to make changes. Thanks so much for carrying through on this visit. It was a gift in every way, and maybe most powerfully in the way it stirred me back to life in my mind. Really, there was never a better friend in any way, than you have been, are being, at this point in my life.

I've worried about transcribing this message, the embarrassing narcissism of the gesture. Look, reader: You see, I really was a good friend. But what I want to highlight is yet something else in friendship stories as I've come to understand them, the phrase: "at this point in my life." Friendship is not only plural—there can be more than two of us in the story—but a matter of timing and doing. To be the friend who would do what was necessary—the task at hand—*when* it was needed. So the gift, of course, lies elsewhere: in Diane's asking me for help, trusting me to bring the book along *then*, not the work itself. This is the gift of friendship that can never be reciprocated: the complete evisceration of the notion of symmetry itself. The thank-you note, therefore, must be mine.

🖾 🖾 🖾

Ten days later, her husband, the man Diane often referred to by his initials, C. D., asked me to fly to San Francisco, where Diane had been hospitalized since her return from England. He was hoping

I'd somehow extract the book from Diane as she lay dying. I knew this was palpably impossible, but I wanted to see her one last time, so I got on the plane.

In the hospital bed, Diane seemed still herself—in moments—but also absorbed with pain management and warding off the constant intrusions of the nurses adjusting her tubes. Despite all evidence that the book would not be finished, C. D. doggedly enlisted a team—Leah, Kate Moses, and me—to sit by Diane's bedside and take notes. We tormented her with our questions, on the *qui vive* for any last revisions she might have in mind. "Finally," I said, looking over our notes, "I think we're done." "Good," she said, closing her eyes. During my final afternoon at the hospital, C. D. was busy on the phone with Diane's editor in New York, asking her to promise to see the book through to completion. He handed the receiver to Diane. She held it to her ear, looking dazed. We could hear the editor weeping.

The last words I heard were the ones Diane uttered to no one in particular, as she dropped the phone into her lap: "This is the pits." The next morning, when I came into her room, I saw that in a penultimate gesture of autonomy, she had pulled out the nose-feeding tube that had been annoying her. She sat, propped up on pillows in the high hospital bed, eyes closed most of the time, her body punctured by drains, floating in and out of lucidity, her delicate face still beautiful.

⌗ ⌗ ⌗

I never had a moment alone with Diane in the hospital room, but I'm not sure what I would have said if I had. She seemed mostly beyond caring, no longer needing anything from us, though we still needed her. She had left us behind. I choked on my good-bye, forcing myself to say the words. I knew when I turned from her bedside to leave the room, we would not speak again. She died a few days after I returned to New York.

FRIENDS IN RETIREMENT

In 2004, not long after Diane had retired from Stanford, she and Elaine Showalter published an epistolary exchange on the subject of retirement in the *Chronicle of Higher Education*. The plan was to discuss whether they had a philosophy of retirement. Almost immediately, prompted by Carolyn's suicide the previous year, Diane explains that she has recently reread Camus's *The Myth of Sisyphus*, a book she hadn't read since college.

The exchange between the two friends was reprinted in the memorial booklet that Diane's friends had put together. "Whatever else 'retiring' means," Diane writes, "it definitely indicates that you are entering the last phase of your life. No one knows when it will end, but everyone knows what will happen." She devotes several paragraphs to her thoughts about Carolyn's suicide, seeing it as an act on Carolyn's part "taken on behalf of what she valued in herself, which was her independence."

I'd never been sure whether Diane and Carolyn had ever met. Carolyn had to have read the Sexton biography, and in Diane's papers I found a typed note from Carolyn about a meeting that Diane had proposed. But Diane evokes having seen Carolyn at my apartment, two years earlier: "Remember how she looked the night of Nancy Miller's book party in November 2002? Carolyn was one of the lionesses."

I have no memory of the three women being present (was Diane in town for a scan?), and, worse still, I've had to work very hard just to reconstruct the party, which must have been for Jane Gallop's *Anecdotal Theory* (she had been invited to speak at the Graduate Center), my *But Enough About Me*, and *Extremities*, an anthology I had co-edited with Jason Tougaw. I waded through my cache of

photographs from the evening, finding Jane Gallop; English Showalter, Elaine's husband; and Kathleen Connor, a young friend of
Diane's and a Plath scholar who happened to be in town and who
offered to make a cake. Neither Elaine, nor Diane, nor Carolyn.
There are, however, several very good pictures of the cake.

Reimagining my living room filled with guests, I picture
Carolyn sitting on our straight-backed armchair, surrounded by
admirers. She must have forgiven me for hurt feelings from our
tiff, because she had no love for parties. ("No one will talk to me;
I'm too old," she'd say, even though a crowd always quickly formed
around her. And then, "I'd have to get dressed up.") Carolyn, the
lioness, but who were the *other* lionesses, if not Elaine and Diane
themselves? It's true that when one expects to be the oldest person
at a gathering—Carolyn's case then, mine now—it's hard not to
foresee being a wallflower. Thanks to the photographs and Diane's
recall, the party has come back to me partially, but it confirms my
unreliability as a narrator, so dependent on the memory of others.
Still, when you are giving a party, you have other things on your
mind (like the cake).

Elaine replied with "almost diametrically opposed feelings and
reactions" to Diane's. What bothered her was not the existential
choice to kill oneself, but the way Carolyn lived in the years leading up to the suicide, the years, in fact, of retirement: "a steady
withdrawal from life, from the trivial, quotidian treats that give
pleasure, and from the tasks and obligations that give pleasure
to others." I want to agree with Diane's view theoretically, since I
believe the feminist logic of "a woman's right to choose," but I find
myself more in agreement emotionally with Elaine's. It was painful
to watch Carolyn narrow her life, which in retrospect looks like a
deliberate preparation for suicide.

▣ ▣ ▣

Diane was seriously ill when she wrote her part of the exchange. In 2004, she began experimental treatments that she hoped would arrest her cancer. She never stopped living her life with a maximum of enjoyment, often pushing her body beyond its limitations because she hated giving up a pleasure. Despite her optimism that some treatment would finally work, I began saving her emails.

At the end of *A Dialogue on Love*, Eve Sedgwick's therapist, Shannon, recalls a session in which Eve described a friend with a "significant depression" and a cancer diagnosis, "someone driven to keep working even if she has no enjoyment in the labor." I recognized Naomi, who was then a colleague of Eve's at Duke, in the portrait. Not being able to stop, despite a lack of enjoyment, had at one time also been a problem for Eve. What she wanted was "someone to tell her she can 'stop now,' e.g., die." That wish had become a voice, Shannon said, that Eve had finally internalized.

I imagine that in the agony of her last days, Diane would have said those words to herself.

Endpieces

ELEGY

> She was my best friend, and she was lending me the brilliance
> of her light in a moment when things were looking decidedly
> dull for me. It was something we did for each other over the
> years, depending on which of us had more light to share at
> the moment.
>
> —Ann Patchett, Afterword to *Autobiography of a Face*.

Ann Patchett and Lucy Grealy met as undergraduates at Sarah
Lawrence, but what was to become their life-long friendship took
root in Iowa City, where both had been accepted at the Iowa Writers'
Workshop for a Master's degree. Ann was planning to be a fiction
writer, Lucy a poet. In *Truth and Beauty*, Patchett recreates the weave
of her friendship with Grealy from the Iowa days to Grealy's death in
2002. "I do not remember our love unfolding," Patchett writes in the
opening chapter of the memoir, "that we got to know one another
and in time became friends. I only remember that she came through
the door and it was there, huge and permanent and first. I felt I had
been chosen by Lucy and I was thrilled."

In a 2007 *Atlantic* interview, when asked how the fact of both
being writers affected their friendship, Patchett explains that the
two "were never writing friends after graduate school. We didn't
really get into each other's work." In this—not getting into each
other's work—Patchett and Grealy lived their friendship along
lines fundamentally different from Kumin and Sexton, whose pact
ensured they shared the production of the work, even though they,
too, distinguished between the kind of writers they were, despite
both being poets. But if Ann and Lucy did not share in each other's
work, Patchett echoes Kumin's claim that she and Sexton had been

"careful" to avoid the destructive feelings of envy and rivalry. As the far more prolific writer of the two, Patchett worked to keep from "making each other feel bad, getting competitive."

She describes in *Truth and Beauty* a moment in their parallel careers in which equilibrium had been attained (and briefly maintained), together or apart:

> Lucy came back to the States in late July to start her residency at Yaddo. . . . I went to Kentucky in the fall, where . . . I had landed a last-minute job teaching literature and fiction writing. . . . Lucy and I both had a place to be, and we had won that place on the strength of our work. I believed there had never been such luck in all the world.

Of course, luck, by definition, is not something one can control; it's always also a matter of timing: "While our plan was always to land the same fellowship at the same time, it never worked out that way. We won the same things but our good luck was always slightly out of sync." This "out-of-syncness" was not, as the story unfolds, simply a matter of "good luck," but rather a constant feature of their friendship, not least because of Lucy's many facial surgeries and her use of drugs. While Kumin acknowledges the differences between herself and Sexton in personality and emotional style, the one more reserved, the other flamboyant, their bond feels in balance, mutual, reciprocal. It is difficult to avoid seeing Ann and Lucy as poignantly mismatched on a number of occasions.

In the memoir, for example, Patchett recounts a scene in which both writers participate in a reading in Provincetown, where they were teaching and living together at the Fine Arts Work Center. Before the event, Ann asks Lucy what she is going to read.

"The tango essay," she replies, then fudging slightly, "It isn't really much about the tango." "I read first," Patchett recalls. "If my life had any learning curve, I knew enough to never to follow Lucy in anything." The Center had been important to both in the years of their apprenticeships; it was where they had written their first books: "To be there together on a clear hot night in July reading from my third book was complete joy," Patchett reflects in retrospect. She also remembers thinking how "funny it was that I was going to hear what [Lucy] had written for the first time, just like every other member of the audience." *Just like every other member of the audience.*

The autobiographical story Lucy reads describes an evening in the East Village during which a woman takes a man back to her apartment to prove that women can have unlimited orgasms and demonstrates this by having seventeen of them as the man watches from the foot of the bed. Patchett writes,

> As I listened, I felt, in no particular order, that I couldn't believe that Lucy had masturbated all night in front of a stranger; I couldn't believe she'd never told me that it had happened; I couldn't believe she'd written about it and then read it to a roomful of strangers on a night that we were reading together. . . .
>
> "You could have told me what you were reading," I said to her on our way to dinner . . .
>
> "Bubala," she said, leaning her head against my shoulder, "you're mad at me."
>
> "Not mad," I lied.
>
> "I've offended your sensibilities," she said. "Forgive me."
>
> I could tell in the darkness from the lilt of her voice that she was pleased.

Not mad, but too hurt to confess the wound, the betrayal, except in retrospect, in memoir. Memoir is a safe place to admit the lies, the reticence that also sustains the contract between friends. In this, contrary to popular opinion, memoir is often truer than life.

In some ways, Patchett's disapproval of Grealy's public persona echoes Kumin's view of Sexton's style. "They were so melodramatic and stagey," Kumin said of Sexton's poetry readings. "I felt they took away from the marvelous texture of the poems by making them into performances. I hated the way Annie pandered to an audience." But unlike Ann, who lies to Lucy, Maxine tells Anne she dislikes the readings, although she also acknowledges, in retrospect, that she herself doesn't know why they bothered her so much. "She and I talked about this lots," Kumin continued. "I mean it wasn't any secret how I felt about it. I loved the poems but I hated to see her do that to them. Now why, I don't know." Perhaps there is always a gap between the privacy of a shared friendship and its public performance. The friend on stage does not coincide completely with the person we think we know and, in some way, think of as ours—uniquely. I'm always surprised when I witness a close friend perform for others, while I'm sitting in the audience, by definition a momentary relegation.

Patchett draws no particular conclusion from this episode, either about her anger over the reading or the refusal to own it. What interests me is just that—the lack of further commentary, or reflection about this difference in sensibility, faced with Lucy's persistent exhibitionism. Again, like Kumin faced with Sexton's emotional demands, Patchett accepts the conditions of her bond with Grealy through another kind of logic:

Lucy didn't just push us all to our limits, which she did, sometimes to our most horrible. She made me realize how much I could love someone, care for someone. Take care of someone. And she really did that for all of us, all of her friends. And it was a wonderful thing. I do not think I would have become as strong of a person had I not known Lucy.

At the end of *Truth and Beauty*, Ann recounts an exchange in a hospital room in which Lucy is recovering from surgery surrounded by friends: "So many of them. So many of us in love with her." And then, a reported conversation: "I'm going to write a book about my friends," Lucy says during a hospital visit. "I have the most extraordinary friends. I've never really understood why everyone has been so good to me, and now I can interview them, talk to them and see." If that wasn't enough to confirm the plural of friends in Lucy's economy, "I'll write a whole chapter about you," she confides. Without missing a beat, Ann replies, accepting the "gift" of the single chapter as reciprocity, "I could write an entire book about you."

"You're such a good friend," Lucy says to Ann after her last surgery. "What did I ever do to deserve a friend like you?"

"You're a good friend to me, too," Ann replies.

"Oh no I'm not. Not like you. . . . But at least I can make you feel like a saint. That's what you've always wanted."

Shocked, Ann looks at her friend lying in her hospital bed. "That's a terrible thing to say."

Lucy is unmoved: "It's true."

Intimacy and the capacity for friendship, Patchett observed in a *New York* magazine profile, were Grealy's particular "gifts": "There are a lot of people who think they're my best friend," Patchett quotes Lucy saying to her, "But you actually are my best friend." Patchett says she figures that Lucy said that to "a lot of people," but, she concludes, "it didn't matter." For Ann, Lucy's extraordinary demands were a kind of reciprocal gift—a gift that made Ann discover that she was capable of this kind of love, maybe also that she needed it. When Maxine Kumin described her friendship with Anne Sexton as being "unbelievable," perhaps part of what she meant was that extraordinary friendships, or friendships with extraordinary people, defy our banal assumptions about the power of these chosen relations to change us. At the end of *Truth and Beauty*, Patchett says that Lucy did not believe that the "most basic rules of life" applied to her and that she herself had come to believe that, too. In the matter of life and death, that turned out to be wrong. In this, Patchett is aligned with Ferrante's Elena Greco, dazzled until the end by her friend's brilliance, despite the workings of fate that might tell a different story.

When Lucy dies from what was probably a heroin overdose, Patchett wishes that she had been there, much as she hated Lucy's attraction to the drug. "Once you realize that you're not going to save someone," Patchett concludes in the *Atlantic* interview, "then all you can do is love them." And unable to save, the novelist resorts to words: "I wrote a book about us. I wrote it as a way to memorialize her and mourn her, and as a way of keeping her own important memoir, *Autobiography of a Face*, alive"—a book in which Ann does not appear—"even as I had not been able to keep her alive."

Truth and Beauty keeps the friendship alive, even when it is absent from Lucy's autobiographical narrative. That's small compensation for loss, but it's not nothing, either.

DIALOGUE IN A GARDEN

This book would never have happened, if it were not for Carolyn
Heilbrun's 1982 Summer Seminar on "The Woman as Hero"....
She changed our lives, and made me, a reprobate Romanticist,
into a feminist scholar.

—Patricia Yaeger, *Honey-Mad Women*

"I've joined the charmed circle," Patsy emailed in April 2013.
"Just got a diagnosis of advanced ovarian cancer. Happily I'm seeing
a surgeon Monday. And I'm hearing that I'll have a good remission.
O brave new world." Cancer was not something I had ever imagined sharing with Patsy, but I was glad, at least, that the diagnosis
to her seemed to come with a ray of hope—"a good remission."
I was impressed that in that mind-shattering moment—the trauma
of diagnosis—she had been able to reach for an ironic grace note,
embracing with a literary touch a prognosis that gave her time.

I had not planned to write about my friendship with Patsy,
but it's been impossible for me not to think of her now, as I
remember the last days of Diane's illness, and also Carolyn's
academic career. In fact, I met Patsy through Carolyn. She had
asked me to speak to her summer seminar about French feminism mainly because Patsy was interested in it. (Carolyn had her
doubts about the subject, though she liked hearing the students,
explicating Luce Irigaray, say "labia" during their oral exams.) My
first impression of Patsy was mediated by Carolyn's description
of her: "She's like Alice in Wonderland." Alice, by virtue of her
very long neck (which we both admired) and her capacity for
wonderment and daring.

Patsy and I had a mantra: Comparison equals death. We practiced comparing ourselves with other women without falling into despair about our inadequacies. We occasionally succeeded, often comparing our situation to Carolyn's. Carolyn, whose professional success was legendary, was invariably our touchstone for analyzing the difficulties of women's lives in academe: "Shared struggle is always better than struggling alone," Patsy wrote after one of our marathon phone sessions, "but also strange and comforting to talk about Carolyn, and much else." After all, it was through Carolyn that our friendship had begun, and if she suffered slights and disappointments, all the more so for us. But if we had met through the web of academic feminism, that's not what kept our bond alive: Talking was.

Patsy died in 2014, despite the good remission she had been promised. Never trust cancer promises.

Patsy's husband, Rich Miller, often posted videos starring Patsy on a website he created for family and friends. One in particular, from a decade or so before the cancer, captures Patsy's playful spirit and, above all, the famous arpeggios of her laughter. Patsy and her colleague Valerie Traub contemplate creating a book together while surveying the state of Patsy's garden, while Rich films and prompts their exchange for the camera:

VAL: I haven't told Patsy yet. I was sitting in an endless meeting and thought what I'd like to do is write a book about gardening with Patsy.

        (Patsy swoons, doing a semi-backbend in assent.)

RICH: What kind of a book?

VAL: A book about what you need to know about gardening that you won't find in any book.

PATSY: I get to be called Sackville; she gets to be called
Vita-West.

VAL: And together we get to be brilliant.

RICH: What are the differences?

VAL: I have a lot more land, but Patsy has a bigger budget.
(Peals of laughter, from both, throughout).

PATSY: She's more fastidious about weeds. I sort of let the
weeds come and go.
(Pan of scruffy patches).

VAL: She's a more big-vision person.
(Gestures).
We both have to deal with dogs. She has to deal with
kids; I don't.

PATSY: I have arthritis.

VAL: I have a bad back.

VAL: She will fall in love with a plant and buy it.

PATSY: And then figure out where to put it.

VAL: I will draw an endless landscape plan and then obsess
about it.

Together we get to be brilliant.

NOTES ON LOSS

> Make new friends, but keep the old. One is silver, the other gold.
> A circle is round, it has no end. That's how long, I will be your
> friend.
>
> —Traditional Girl Scout song

I remember little from my childhood, but the lyrics from that Girl
Scout song have always stuck in my head. Actually, I remembered
only the first two lines; the rest I looked up. Why the song should be
part of Girl Scout ritual, or lodged in my memory, I do not know,
not least because I did not love scouting (the uniforms were a bilious
green, and we had to learn how to sew). It feels strange, I find, to make
new friends when one is old; unlike the circle in the song, the future is
not an unbroken line. I want to finish this book before there are more
friends to miss and to mourn.

Mourning, of course, is a way of keeping a bond with the past.
In *Men in Dark Times*, through the portrait of a friend, Hannah
Arendt identifies the urgency behind keeping the memories of
friends alive:

> As he grew older, it was only natural that the number of dead
> friends should increase; and although I never saw him violently
> stricken with grief, I was aware of the almost calculated careful-
> ness with which he kept mentioning their names as though he
> were afraid that through some fault of his they would slip away
> altogether from the company of the living.

We keep those names in the "company of the living," since we
want still to live with them, even if it's hard not to feel a little

melancholy keeping company with the dead. And, of course, though trickier to admit, we can also hope our friends among the living will want to continue to live with us when we are gone. Naming them is the easy part.

What about now, making friends in late life? Here's Diana Athill on the subject at ninety-three, describing her reluctant move from a house she loved to a room (of her own, but just the one room) in a home for the elderly:

> Old-age friendships are slightly different from those made in the past, which consisted largely of sharing whatever happened to be going on. What happens to be going on for us now is waiting to die, which is of course a bond of a sort, but lacks the element of enjoyability necessary to friendship. In my current friendships I find that element not in our present circumstances but in excursions into each other's pasts.

I read these lines with the shiver of amazement that only something new can produce in *Alive, Alive Oh! And Other Things That Matter*. I had picked up the collection of personal essays by chance in a bookstore one summer while visiting London, drawn in by the striking portrait of its author on the cover, a beautiful, vibrant woman.

At seventy-five and already feeling old—a state Athill postponed fully embracing until her nineties—I suddenly saw how much my idea of life in one's later years had been shaped by Carolyn's ambivalent stance on aging. On the one hand, in *The Last Gift of Time*, Carolyn describes the peculiar beauty of feeling life ebbing—the poignant sense of doing some things for the last time in one's sixties, the excitement of being free of the burdens of conventional femininity. But on the other, that frame of mind was made possible only by the conviction that she did not plan to advance much further into the more vulnerable zones of old age. In fact, Carolyn's perspective on aging depended on the decision—very different from Athill's turn toward a new way of living—to end her life at some point in her seventies, at seventy-seven, as it turned out. Her suicide has loomed as both warning and invitation, despite the fact that I have two great friends, Mary Ann Caws and Alix Kates Shulman, writers well into their eighties, who embrace aging and life with Athill's zest. After the cancer diagnosis that inaugurated my seventies, I assumed the disease would make the question of how to live in old age moot. I confess that I almost liked the idea that the end of my life would be decided for me by cancer, rather than depression. Seven years later, however, two surgeries on, it's still "Alive, Alive Oh!"

What particularly captured my attention in Athill's reflection on old age was her vision of friendships formed in such advanced age with the women in her new home. Since I'm not in my nineties, and that decade not plausibly on my horizon, what intrigued me was the notion of forging different kinds of friendship narratives in the distinctly unenjoyable, un-longed-for perspective of death Athill describes. In the place of friendships we've lived with others, a shared history, we can discover in the silver friendships formed in old age the pasts of people one does not already know, undoing the conventional expectations of tenses, with more delight than sorrow—and, notably, make friendships in the plural.

So, what does making new friends mean to me now, neither scout nor splendid old-lady writer with a sanguine temperament? This is where the best-friend question comes in.

Last spring, my ten-year-old goddaughter, Hannah, was visiting for the afternoon. She was visibly drooping, though naturally not too tired for shoe shopping, our seasonal ritual. The sleep part of the sleepover she had had the night before clearly had been minimal. I asked Hannah whether Jill, her sleepover date, was her best friend. She shot me the withering look adults deserve when they ask dumb questions. "I have other best friends," she said. But a best friend is singular. How can you have more than one "best"? I refrained from asking. This was wisdom I needed to ponder. Could it apply to a septuagenarian?

Naomi said she never made another friend like me. That remark, shared by her widower, seemed true equally for me, I wrote earlier, and sad. But while that is, on the face of it, a rather melancholy fact, I'm not sure now whether I fully regret not having that kind of friend. Perhaps this is why Ferrante's novels pierced me as they did, with the indelible portrait they offered of a friendship between women whose flame burned so brightly it inevitably became extinguished, a too-muchness of need and identification that crashed into a story with a joyless ending, a story, a fiction about how that might happen.

Is it odd, then, that one of the more interesting books about women's friendship should focus on the demise of relationships, rather than their celebration? *The Friend Who Got Away* is an anthology of autobiographical essays about friendships between women that ended, usually badly. The book opens with an epigraph from Virginia Woolf: "I have lost friends, some by death . . . others through sheer inability to cross the street." The line (spoken by the character Bernard in *The Waves*) captures for me the painful, unexpected, even devastating aspect of friendship's failures: neither death nor disaster but rather a distinct distancing, a moving away, as it were, without movement. I, too, have lost friends by death—those I remember in this book, and others from precisely what Woolf describes: the "sheer inability to cross the street." An act of passivity, inertia with the force of a blow.

And when the friend tires of you, it feels as if you've been knocked out. After I was dropped by a friend to whom I had felt intensely bonded over a matter of years, despite the fact of geographical separation (she lived in Paris, I in New York), I was in equal parts mortified and mystified. It was September 1989. I had just settled in to a sabbatical year in Paris and was excited by the possibility that C. and I would now see each other more often than the haphazard meetings we typically had in one city or the other, sometimes from one year to the next. That fall, we met at what we had always called "our" café and entertained each other, I thought, with our usual banter. But when we parted, C. said nothing about another date. I never heard from her again, nor did she return my calls. Was it something I said?

After weeks of silence, I had to conclude that I no longer interested C.

⊞ ⊞ ⊞

There are clearer friendship breakup models, of course: the friend says something so cruel as to be unforgivable. Or the friend reveals a morally unattractive "double face" you cannot countenance. Or, distance and circumstances make intimacy harder to sustain, so you give in to laziness. You discover that your friendship was situational, as people say some depressions are. What's harder to understand is why, if the perfectly nice friend does not commit, on the face of it an unpardonable act, you cut your ties with her. Here's where the two sides of friendship take on new meaning.

The break occurs when you are suddenly brought up short by her B-side. It's not as though her B-side wasn't always there. But now you hear only the B-side playing. The hardest part about this kind of falling-out is that it cannot easily be put into words. After all, is it her fault that she's what she's always been? "I have neither the courage to lie to her," Elizabeth Strout writes in an essay about a failed friendship, "nor the courage to tell her the truth."

It does not follow, of course, that because you've been dumped without having been told why (this is where breaking up with a lover for a sexual betrayal is strangely easier to bear), this constitutes justification for doing just that to another. It does not excuse the consequences of the act. For what you have to hear in Woolf's phrase is the finality of "sheer"—the recognition that the friendship, like a piece of fine china, has broken into too many pieces to put back together. I still live, in bewildered memory, thirty years later, the shattering of what I shared with C., our golden bowl, and so it pains me to acknowledge that I have also been C.

Still, friendship is based on affinity, and choice. So why shouldn't one be able to unchoose? And why presume that friendship should last forever? The difficulty of unchoosing inheres in the ethics of friendship, the logic of affinity, of election.

We change over time, and—why should this be surprising?—we do not necessarily change in the same way, in the same direction. Time inflects distance. The perception of change is rarely symmetrical, almost never mutual—if it was, there would be no need for rupture. Rather, as Cicero wisely suggested, "Our care should be that the friendships appear to have burned out rather than to have been stamped out."

How to avoid the catastrophe? In theory, if you were to say, when you start to have the feeling of no longer being attuned, no longer hearing the music of friendship—"Look, this isn't working,

I feel X about you, you seem to feel Y about me"—shouldn't that prevent going past the brink, over the cliff of withdrawal? Yes, but once you have that feeling, it is already too late. The spell is broken, and you won't want to "work on" the relationship—not having to work is the charm of friendship. Friendships thrive on their own form of magic, and once the spell is broken, there is no mending.

Perhaps it's sour grapes, but I don't yearn for another best friend, or rather, to be more truthful, I no longer want one because I'm not capable of being one. Maybe it's time to suspect that the best friend as pictured by the ancients was always only a fantasy, a perfect match of longing, not suited to the contemporary psychology of mirrored emotions, the kinds of volatile affection lived by imperfect beings. That doesn't mean that we moderns don't keep trying: BFFs, "besties," the language won't let go.

Sexton and Kumin, pals of the desk, pals of the heart, telephone buddies. Caldwell again: "It's an old, old story: I had a friend and we shared everything, and then she died and so we shared that." That old story is behind me. There is no one with whom I can share everything. "Conspirators. Emotional business partners," as Lorrie Moore puts it in *Who Will Run the Frog Hospital?*, her novel of girls bonding. Now, for me, the sharing is parceled out among friends. Belatedly, I realize that this has always been true. After all, there were friends I shared with Naomi, and friends with whom I talked about her, and still do. She was, almost until the end, the special friend, and certainly in memory, the best, I'm willing to say.

Naomi collected plates, usually nineteenth-century majolica, often featuring a design of molded colorful vegetables. Once, it must have been in the seventies, she brought me back from France a plate of my own, not majolica but a 1930s French hand-painted plate with scalloped edges, wired for hanging. Two lines of blue cursive script inscribed the kind of message found in Chinese fortune cookies: "La fumée s'envole, l'amitié reste." Smoke vanishes, friendship remains. I hung the plate on a wall flanked by two of her father's prints. During the period of our estrangement, I had to take the plate down. The irony of the message was too painful a reminder of what had been, the embers still hot. After our reunion and just before her death, I rehung the plate.

▯ ▯ ▯

I have two memorial booklets, one from Carolyn's "Service of Remembrance," held a week after her death, and one of Diane's "Memories by Her Friends," reflections from the Women Writers' Salon she founded in London in 2003, compiled four years after she died. (The third, Naomi's, no surprise, is missing.) The booklets make for bittersweet reading. But what's striking about them is how, in each case, the portraits of the women that emerge from several friends are consistent. Carolyn, a woman with strong opinions, feminist and literary (or both at the same time), and specific habits and tastes, remarked upon by all: walking, talking, eating (or some combination of those), drinking, supporting other women, taking unpopular positions, being unwaveringly loyal to her friends. At the same time, many of us were angry and felt betrayed by the suicide; anger ran through the stories like a dark thread. The language of the remembrances radiated the shock of the event. Diane's booklet was created several years after her death, when we all had had time to dwell on our loss and move toward elegy. We remembered: her boldness, her generosity, her hospitality, her openness, her exuberance, her poise, the poise of her intelligence, her beauty and style, her passion for biography, her belief in others, her joyful stance toward life, even when seriously ill. But both had the art of making their friends feel special, valued, and loved. They lived their friendships in the plural, and when you were with them, you were the friend they wanted.

I'm looking for a metaphor on which to end, not "alive, alive oh," but something at least pointing in that direction. I can borrow one from Colette, another woman writer who enjoyed life in all its variety, including growing old, and who, like Athill, never stopped writing. It's from the end of a novel in which "Colette" (the writer's avatar) describes the departure of her current lover. She helps him leave by conjuring his transformation into many forms, finally by imagining his place in "an unending book" whose still-open pages she might yet fill, an oasis, a pause, perhaps a reprieve from an absolute ending.

This book is my reprieve.

Notes

I. CAROLYN HEILBRUN

9   "Aging set me free": Carolyn G. Heilbrun, foreword to *A Certain Age: Reflecting on Menopause*, ed. Nancy K. Miller and Carolyn G. Heilbrun (New York: Columbia University Press, 1994), xvi. Originally published as *A Certain Age: Reflecting on the Menopause*, ed. Joanna Goldsworthy (London: Virago, 1993).

11   "I will wager": Heilbrun, *A Certain Age*, xv.

12   "Feminism, humanism": Heilbrun, *A Certain Age*, xvi.

13   "The answer": Heilbrun, *A Certain Age*, xv.

13   "I have three children": Heilbrun, *A Certain Age*, xv–xvi.

15   "He had believed in me"; "Friendship is plainer": Paul Theroux, *Sir Vidia's Shadow: A Friendship Across Five Continents* (New York: Mariner, 1998), 99.

15   Vidia dumped Paul: The two men reconciled after a fifteen-year silence at the Hay Festival in 2011.

20   "It was easy": Tama Janowitz, "Engagements," *The New Yorker*, September 2, 1985, 30.

20   "I was sitting": Janowitz, 32.

20   "The teacher, Anna Castleton": Janowitz, 32.

21   "Status of empirical discourse": Janowitz, 32.

21   "Without using 'class,' she argued": Janowitz, 32.

22   "I wondered whether": Janowitz, 33.

22   "Beaver, paddling frantically": Janowitz, 33.

22   "I had hoped to please": Janowitz, 33.

23   "Had fallen prey": Janowitz, 33.

27   "Friend is, as we assert, a second self": Aristotle, *The Works of Aristotle*, trans. W. D. Ross (Oxford: Clarendon, 1915), Book II, 15, Line 1213a.

27   "When a man thinks of a true friend": Cicero, *On the Good Life*, trans. Michael Grant (London: Penguin, 1971), 189.

27   "As it were, another self": Cicero, *On Old Age, On Friendship, On Divination*, trans. W. A. Falconer (Cambridge, MA: Harvard University Press, 1923), 189.

27   Create self-knowledge: Ivy Schweitzer, *Perfecting Friendship: Politics and Affiliation in Early American Literature* (Chapel Hill: University of North Carolina Press, 2006), 36. See the introduction and passim for the importance of Aristotle and the tradition as revised by women writers.

28   "Because it was he"; "gathering in the city"; "taken with each other": Montaigne, *The Complete Essays of Montaigne*, trans. Donald M. Frame (Stanford, CA: Stanford University Press, 1957), 139.

28   "I was already so formed": Montaigne, 143.

28   Friendship's "double face"; "even the best of friendships": Alexander Nehamas, *On Friendship* (New York: Basic Books, 2016), 6.

28   "Dangers and disappointments": Nehamas, 7.

28   "May actually be the other face"; "Pleasures and benefits": Nehamas, 8.

28   "Friendship and immorality": Nehamas, 189.

30   "Untold story of friendship": Carolyn G. Heilbrun, *Writing a Woman's Life* (New York: Ballantine, 1988), 98.

30   "A constant and continuous dialogue": Heilbrun, *Writing a Woman's Life*, 99.

30   "It's an old, old story": Gail Caldwell, *Let's Take the Long Way Home: A Memoir of Friendship* (New York: Random House, 2010), 3.

32   "I experienced my need": Carolyn G. Heilbrun, *The Last Gift of Time* (New York: Dial, 1997), 27.

32   Friend and biographer, Susan Kress: (Personal Communication). See also Susan Kress, *Carolyn G. Heilbrun: Feminist in a Tenured Position* (Charlottesville: University of Virginia Press, 1997).

32   "Of course there is always a price": Heilbrun, *The Last Gift of Time*, 35.

33   "The heart breaks open": Caldwell, 182.

33   "Caroline's death was a vacancy": Caldwell, 161.

34   "I, being fat, dislike thin women": Amanda Cross [Carolyn G. Heilbrun], *Honest Doubt* (New York: Ballantine, 2000), 2.

35   "What was soon obvious": Heilbrun, *The Last Gift of Time*, 128.

35   "Free individuals from the prison of gender": Heilbrun, *The Last Gift of Time*, 135.

35   "Androgynous self": Heilbrun, *The Last Gift of Time*, 133.

35   She went on to say: Morris Beja to Carolyn G. Heilbrun. (Personal Communication)

36 "I've got to admit": Cross, 7.

36 "I put my hands": Cross, 8.

36 "I walked over": Cross, 17.

37 "I like a *big* dog": Caldwell, 182.

39 "There are four ways to write a woman's life": Heilbrun, *Writing a Woman's Life*, 11.

40 "The woman herself may tell it": Heilbrun, *Writing a Woman's Life*, 11.

40 "All the conscious reasons": Heilbrun, *Writing a Woman's Life*, 120.

41 "Detritus of the mind": Heilbrun, *The Last Gift of Time*, 120.

41 "I sought, I guess": Heilbrun, *Writing a Woman's Life*, 114–15.

42 "By the time I'd finished reading"; "*Is this what I've been doing*": Kate Bolick, *Spinster: Making a Life of One's Own* (New York: Crown, 2015), 159.

42 "Created the pages that were my life": Bolick, 160.

42 "Spinster wish"; "Avenues of meaning and identity"; "Wonderful term": Bolick, 286.

43 "Such is the odd fate": Bolick, 159. A recent look at Heilbrun's career updates Bolick's evaluation even further. See Judith Pascoe, "Carolyn Heilbrun Told You So," *Public Books*, September 7, 2018, http://www.publicbooks.org/carolyn-heilbrun-told-you-so/

43 "Secrecy is power": Heilbrun, *Writing a Woman's Life*, 116.

47 In *affidamento*. "*affidamento* places emphasis not on a given similarity between women but rather on the specificity of each woman and on differences among women." Leslie Elwell, "Breaking Bonds: Refiguring Maternity in Elena Ferrante's *The Lost Daughter*." In *The Works of Elena Ferrante: Reconfiguring the Margins*, ed. Grace Russo Bullaro and Stephanie V. Love (New York: Palgrave Macmillan, 2016), 243.

50 "What is this?": Mary McCarthy, "Saying Good-by to Hannah," *New York Review of Books*, January 22, 1976, www.nybooks.com/articles/1976/01/22/saying-good-by-to-hannah/.

50 "Liked gifts": Kress, 9.

51 "Put no pictures on the walls": Heilbrun, *The Last Gift of Time*, 19.

54 The *Times* ran a story: Karen W. Arenson, "Columbia Soothes the Dogs of War in Its English Dept." *New York Times*, March 17, 2002, www.nytimes.com/2002/03/17/nyregion/columbia-soothes-the-dogs-of-war-in-its-english-dept.html.

54 "In a huff": Arenson.

54 "Seemed to imply": Carolyn G. Heilbrun, letter to the editor, "'Huff,' Deconstructed," *New York Times*, March 20, 2002, www.nytimes.com/2002/03/20/opinion/l-huff-deconstructed-143634.html.

58   "All the children climbed out"; "To be excluded": Roland Barthes, *Roland Barthes by Roland Barthes*, trans. Richard Howard (New York: Farrar, Straus and Giroux, 1977), 121.

59   "Finding yourself in a hole": Carolyn G. Heilbrun, "Taking a U-Turn: The Aging Woman as Explorer of New Territory," *Women's Review of Books* 20, no. 10/11 (July 2003): 18–19.

59   "Without the slightest subject for a book": Margaret Atwood, *Negotiating with the Dead: A Writer on Writing* (Cambridge: Cambridge University Press, 2002), xiii.

59   "A vast emptiness": Marguerite Duras, *Writing* (Minneapolis: University of Minnesota Press, 2011), 7.

59   "To be alone with the as yet unwritten book": Duras, 15.

60   "I must write": Heilbrun, "Taking a U-Turn," 18.

61   "Looking back": Carolyn G. Heilbrun, *When Men Were the Only Models We Had: My Teachers, Fadiman, Barzun, Trilling* (Philadelphia: University of Pennsylvania Press, 2002), 143.

68   "Determination": Heilbrun, *The Last Gift of Life*, 8.

68   "Each day one can say": Heilbrun, *The Last Gift of Life*, 10.

69   "Rereading is much recommended": Carolyn G. Heilbrun, "Guest Column: From Rereading to Reading." *PMLA* 119, no. 2 (March 2004): 211.

69   "Why is life so tragic": Virginia Woolf, *The Diary of Virginia Woolf*, vol. 3, ed. Anne Olivier Bell and Andrew McNeillie (New York: Harvest, 1980), 72.

70   "As a cloud": Virginia Woolf, *Mrs. Dalloway* (New York: Harcourt, 1953), 74–75.

70   "Pinker": Woolf, *Diary*, vol. 3, 233.

70   "Now time must not": Woolf, *Diary*, vol. 3, 234.

71   "And so I pitched": Woolf, *Diary*, vol. 3, 234–35.

71   "And as usual": Woolf, *Diary*, vol. 3, 235.

71   "The sail filled out again": Woolf, *Diary*, vol. 3, 235.

72   "She chose to end"; "Having totted up the score": Carolyn G. Heilbrun, "Virginia Woolf in Her Fifties," *Hamlet's Mother and Other Women* (New York: Columbia University Press, 1990), 93.

73   "Writing a Feminist's Life: Academics and Their Memoirs": "Writing a Feminist's Life: Academics and Their Memoirs," conference held at Columbia University, New York, NY, February 11, 2005.

73   A piece composed in response to: Gayle Greene and Coppélia Kahn, eds., *Changing Subjects: The Making of Feminist Literary Criticism* (London: Routledge, 1993), 2.

74   "To me, roughly a decade": Carolyn G. Heilbrun, afterword to *Changing Subjects: The Making of Feminist Literary Criticism*, ed. Gayle Green and Coppélia Kahn (London: Routledge, 1993), 267.

75 "Columbia has stopped": Heilbrun, afterword to *Changing Subjects*, 270.

77 "Out of hating range": *The Woman Warrior: Memoirs of a Girlhood Among Ghosts* (New York: Vintage, 1989), 52.

78 "Spiritless, wan, and remote"; "As if Florence was breaking up with her": Brian Morton, *Florence Gordon* (New York: Houghton Mifflin Harcourt, 2014), 270.

II. NAOMI SCHOR

81 Yiyun Li borrows the sentence in the title of her memoir from Katherine Mansfield's *Notebooks, Complete Edition*, ed. Margaret Scott (Minneapolis: University of Minnesota, 2002), 222.

86 "There was something intangible": Gail Caldwell, *Let's Take the Long Way Home: A Memoir of Friendship* (New York: Random House, 2010), 12.

87 "We'll see who wins": Ferrante, *My Brilliant Friend*, 1, 273.

88 "You're my brilliant friend": Ferrante, *My Brilliant Friend*, 1, 312.

88 "I *want* you to do better": Ferrante, *My Brilliant Friend*, 3, 273.

88 "Mirror . . . inabilities": Ferrante, *My Brilliant Friend*, 3, 274.

90 "Memories are what": Joan Didion, *Blue Nights* (New York: Knopf, 2011), 64.

91 "Consciousness": Vivian Gornick, "Consciousness," *New York Times*, January 10, 1971, www.nytimes.com/1971/01/10/archives/consciousness-consciousness.html.

112 "Because we had known"; "Finally I blurted out": Caldwell, 27.

112 "What a swampland": Caldwell, 28.

113 "Oh no": Caldwell, 28.

113 "She would say": Caldwell, 29.

113 "That's what was wrong": Simone de Beauvoir, *Memoirs of a Dutiful Daughter*, trans. James Kirkup (New York: Penguin, 1959), 95.

114 "Zaza was my best friend": Beauvoir, 94.

126 "To think that I've": Marcel Proust, *Remembrance of Things Past*, trans. C. K. Scott Moncrieff, vol. 1 (New York: Vintage, 1982), 415.

127 "A woman is like a book": Serge Doubrovsky, *Un amour de soi* (Paris: Hachette, 1982), 351; my translation.

127 "This way you won't regret": Doubrovsky, 375.

128 "The two of them": Doubrovsky, 177–78.

132 "United by friendship": Cicero, "Laelius: On Friendship," in *On the Good Life*, trans. Michael Grant (London: Penguin, 1971), 189.

136 "It is time for me to get personal"; "Critic of nineteenth-century": Naomi Schor, *Bad Objects: Essays Popular and Unpopular* (Durham, NC: Duke University Press, 1995), ix.

136 "Melancholic disposition"; "We, the now middle-aged": Schor, *Bad Objects*, 159.

137 "Now that I'm close to": Elena Ferrante, *The Story of the Lost Child*, trans. Ann Goldstein (New York: Europa, 2015), 25.

140 "I've finished this story": Ferrante, *The Story of the Lost Child*, 469.

140 "So I had to acknowledge": Ferrante, *The Story of the Lost Child*, 464.

140 "We was girls together": Toni Morrison, *Sula* (New York: Plume, 1973), 174.

140 "Friendship between women": Toni Morrison, "The Site of Memory," in *Inventing the Truth: The Art and Craft of Memoir*, ed. William Zinsser (New York: Houghton Mifflin, 1995), 96.

145 "One always leaves before the other": Jacques Derrida, *The Work of Mourning*, trans. Pascale-Anne Brault and Michael Naas (Chicago: University of Chicago Press, 2001), 1. The translators and editors of Derrida's work on friendship and mourning summarize his thinking about the inevitability of losing a friend in the introduction to this book. The last time I saw Derrida, he was enjoying a brief remission from pancreatic cancer. He died in 2004, not long after having written his last farewell to friends.

III. DIANE MIDDLEBROOK

155 "I stopped at the door to the room": Joan Didion, *The Year of Magical Thinking* (New York: Knopf, 2005), 37.

156 "As the world knows": Maxine Kumin, "A Friendship Remembered," in *Anne Sexton: The Artist and Her Critics*, ed. J. D. McClatchy (Bloomington: Indiana University Press, 1978), 103.

156 "After Sexton built": Diane Wood Middlebrook, *Anne Sexton: A Biography* (New York: Vintage, 1992), 142.

156 "We sometimes connected": Kumin, "A Friendship Remembered," 103.

157 "Isn't it true": Nancy K. Miller, Maxine Kumin, and Diane Middlebrook, "Remembering Anne Sexton: Maxine Kumin in Conversation with Diane Middlebrook," *PMLA* 127, no. 2 (March 2012): 293.

158 "I met Maxine Kumin": Anne Sexton, "The Art of Poetry: Anne Sexton," in *Anne Sexton: The Artist and Her Critics*, 7.

158 "On that second line": Ellen Goodman and Patricia O'Brien, *I Know Just What You Mean: The Power of Friendship in Women's Lives* (New York: Fireside, 2000), 42.

158 "Kumin had companions": Carolyn G. Heilbrun, *The Last Gift of Time* (New York: Dial, 1997), 141–42.

159 "Unmet friend": Heilbrun, 138.

159 "Many friends personally known": Heilbrun, 149.

159 "Awkward, considered intellectual": Heilbrun, 140.

160 "Diane's genius was for friendship": Kate Moses, "Narrative Magazine Friday Feature: Kate Moses's 'Chocolate Cake for Diane,'" *Huffington Post*, August 12, 2011, www.huffingtonpost.com/2011/08/12/narrative-magazine-friday_n_924924 .html.

161 "Our partnership": Moses.

162 "A close personal friend": Maxine Kumin, "With Martha George Meek," in *To Make a Prairie: Essays on Poets, Poetry, and Country Living* (Ann Arbor: University of Michigan Press, 1979), 29.

163 "Could any act of reciprocity": Lyndall Gordon, *Shared Lives: Growing Up in 50s Cape Town* (London: Virago, 1992), 295.

164 A reciprocal relation: I'm tempted to call the power of this exchange "female amity," borrowing, while slightly short-circuiting, Sharon Marcus's definition of friendship between women in Victorian novels. Sharon Marcus, *Between Women: Friendship, Desire, and Marriage in Victorian England* (Princeton, NJ: Princeton University Press, 2007), 82–83. In *Like Subjects, Love Objects: Essays on Recognition and Sexual Difference* (New Haven, CT: Yale University Press, 1995), Jessica Benjamin incisively analyzes this form of intersubjectivity as a process described as "mutual recognition" (20–22).

166 "But I feel I was lucky to have her"; "Yes, and that was a lot": Miller, Kumin, and Middlebrook, 293.

167 "Symbolically . . . represent[s]": Deborah Tannen, *You Were Always Mom's Favorite: Sisters in Conversation Throughout Their Lives* (New York: Ballantine, 2010), 14.

167 "A friend might stop being": Tannen, 24.

167 "I never had a sister": Miller, Kumin, and Middlebrook, 293.

167 "Friends are the sisters we were meant to have": Tannen, 9.

167 "You would leave the phone open"; "I was much more reserved"; "Does this sound good?": Miller, Kumin, and Middlebrook, 293.

168 "We were careful not to compete"; "I never had a sister": Miller, Kumin, and Middlebrook, 293.

168 "Max and I say": Middlebrook, 142.

168 "The cline of person": A. L. Becker, quoted in Tannen, 36.

168 Close and distant: Tannen, 36–37.

169 "Ugly sisters": Tannen, 13.

169 "A back and forth, a continual negotiation": Tannen, 99–100.

170 "We were more or less the same dress size"; "But we had dresses": Miller, Kumin, and Middlebrook, 296.

170 "The striking ways in which": Middlebrook, 284.

171 "She was very demanding": Miller, Kumin, and Middlebrook, 296.

172 "Really, there was no other"; "She felt that the poems": Miller, Kumin, and Middlebrook, 298.

173 "She actually was still working on things": Miller, Kumin, and Middlebrook, 298.

173 "On loan to poetry": Kumin, "A Friendship Remembered," 92.

187 "Whatever else 'retiring' means"; "Taken on behalf"; "Remember how she looked": Elaine Showalter and Diane Middlebrook, "Book Salons, Hormones, and Online Hate Mail: A Post-retirement Conversation," *Chronicle of Higher Education*, February 27, 2004, www.chronicle.com/article/Book-Salons-Hormones -and/31889.

188 "Almost diametrically opposed"; "A steady withdrawal": Showalter and Middlebrook.

189 "Significant depression": Eve Kosofsky Sedgwick, *A Dialogue on Love* (Boston: Beacon, 1999), 220.

ENDPIECES

Elegy

193 Lucy, a poet: *Autobiography of a Face*, Grealy's hugely successful 1994 memoir, narrates her history as a cancer survivor. As a child, she had Ewing's sarcoma, which led to a series of reconstructive surgeries to repair the damage to her jaw caused by the cancer. In her memoir, Patchett describes what the severe facial disfigurement meant psychologically for Lucy: "She was trapped in a room full of mirrors, and every direction she looked in she saw herself, her face, her loneliness." Ann Patchett, *Truth and Beauty* (New York: HarperCollins, 2004), 171.

193 "I do not remember": Patchett, 7.

193 "Were never writing friends": Abigail Cutler, "My Pornography," *The Atlantic*, July 2007, www.theatlantic.com/magazine/archive/2007/07/my-pornography /306068/.

194 "Lucy came back": Patchett, 89.

194 "While our plan": Patchett, 103.

195 "The tango essay"; "To be there together": Patchett, 160.

195 "As I listened": Patchett, 162.

196 "They were so melodramatic and stagey": Middlebrook, 306.

196 "She and I talked about this lots": Maxine Kumin, unpublished interview with Diane Middlebrook, October 9, 1980.

197   "Lucy didn't just push us all to our limits": Cutler.

197   "So many of them"; "I'm going to write": Patchett, 227.

197   "You're such a good friend": Patchett, 225.

198   "There are a lot of people": Ann Patchett, "The Face of Pain," *New York Magazine*, http://nymag.com/nymetro/news/people/features/n_8396/index1.html.

198   "Once you realize that you're not going to save someone": Cutler.

Dialogue in a Garden

199   "This book would never": Patricia S. Yaeger, *Honey-Mad Women: Emancipatory Strategies in Women's Writing* (New York: Columbia University Press, 1988). *Honey-Mad Women* was the seventh book, and Yaeger's first, to appear in the Gender and Culture Series.

Notes on Loss

202   "As he grew older": Hannah Arendt, *Men in Dark Times* (New York: Harvest, 1968), 254.

203   "Old-age friendships": Diana Athill, *Alive, Alive Oh! And Other Things That Matter* (London: Granta, 2016), 113.

205   "I have lost friends": Virginia Woolf, epigraph to *The Friend Who Got Away: Twenty Women's True Life Tales of Friendships that Blew Up, Burned Out or Faded Away*, ed. Jenny Offill and Elissa Schappell (New York: Broadway, 2005).

207   "I have neither the courage": Elizabeth Strout, "Toads and Snakes," in *The Friend Who Got Away*, ed. Offill and Schappell, 90.

207   "Our care should be": Cicero, *On Old Age, On Friendship, On Divination*, trans. W. A. Falconer (Cambridge, MA: Harvard University Press), 187.

208   The language won't let go: See Natalie Angier's "You Share Everything With Your Bestie. Even Brain Waves," https://nyti.ms/2JoPogX. The print version features two women holding hands with brain waves intertwined. The sense of longing for a best friend and celebrating the need for that connection animates a 2018 book about female friendship by Kayleen Schaefer, *Text Me When You Get Home: The Evolution and Triumph of Modern Female Friendship* (New York: Dutton, 2018). Schaefer's research takes her back to the nineteenth century through Sharon Marcus's excellent academic study *Between Women: Friendship, Desire, and Marriage in Victorian England* (Princeton, NJ: Princeton

University Press, 2007), as if the twentieth century had never happened as a result of a bizarre form of collective amnesia. "This book is about the validation—and celebration—of our friendships, but it's only a start. The conversation about how important other women can be in our lives has just begun" (Schaefer, 10).

208   "It's an old, old story": Caldwell, 3.

208   "Conspirators. Emotional business partners": Lorrie Moore, *Who Will Run the Frog Hospital?* (New York: Knopf, 1994), 38.

210   In an unending book: Colette, *Break of Day*, trans. Enid McLeod (New York: Farrar, Straus and Giroux, 1961), 143.

Acknowledgments

This is a book about friendship and not surprisingly many friends have played a role in bringing the book to completion. I am especially grateful to Marissa Brostoff, Laura Frost, Susan Gubar, Tahneer Oksman, and Victoria Rosner for their generous and critical readings of the manuscript in its various stages. I also am grateful to Sandy Petrey, my brilliant husband and fiercest critic, for his revision of the final version.

These are not my only debts. Jacob Aplaca gracefully rose to the challenge of organizing the ridiculous number of citations and proved to be a fabulous editorial assistant. Leah Middlebrook was kind enough to grant me permission to quote fully from her mother's beautiful emails. My agent Cecelia Cancellaro has supported the project from its inception. I am particularly indebted to Jennifer Crewe, Associate Provost and Director of Columbia University Press, for vetting the manuscript with her characteristic finesse.

Jojo Karlin's wonderful drawings are an unexpected gift now inseparable from the book itself.

I thank the Bogliasco Foundation for the residency that enabled me to begin the book.

I also need to say, of course, how much I love my friends (and I include here my students), who, as Hannah Arendt put it, make life worth living. This book is for them, even if their names are not in it.

Above all, posthumous gratitude to Carolyn Heilbrun, Diane Middlebrook, and Naomi Schor, whose friendships are the book.

Earlier versions of the book's chapters appeared in the following journals and are used here with permission: "On Being Wrong." *Profession 2008.* 54-65. "A Feminist Friendship Archive." *Profession 2011.* MLA, 2011: 68-76. "Remembering Anne Sexton: Maxine Kumin in Conversation with Diane Middlebrook." *PMLA* 127, no. 2 (2012): 292-300. "Elegiac Friendship: Notes on Loss." *Feminist Studies.* Special Issue: Women's Friendships. 42, no. 2 (2016): 426-44.

GENDER AND CULTURE

A Series of Columbia University Press

Nancy K. Miller and Victoria Rosner, Series Editors

Carolyn G. Heilbrun (1926-2003) and Nancy K. Miller, Founding Editors